THE
DIAKONATE

SERVANT — LEADERS

by

Dale Rumble

"Called to Serve, Discipled to Lead"

Here is a fresh look at the Church that is being restored and built for the end times. We will see how home churches and servant leaders are being raised up to provide a quality of body life that will enable the Church to be victorious in the coming days of shaking and tribulation.

Destiny Image Publishers
P.O. Box 351
Shippensburg, PA 17257

"Speaking to the Purposes of God for this Generation"

ISBN 1-56043-020-6

For Worldwide Distribution
Printed in the U.S.A.

| First Printing: | 1990 |
| Second Printing: | 1993 |

Dedication

This book is dedicated to all those who serve in the house of the Lord and, in particular, to the men with whom I am yoked in eldership.

"Unless the Lord builds the house, they labor in vain who build it..."

Psalm 127:1

Special thanks to:

— Phyllis Murphy and Joan Colao, who so faithfully and carefully typed the manuscript.

— My dear wife, Bertha, whose patience and loving support have encouraged me in the Lord.

Contents

Foreword

We live in a day when information abounds. Never in history have there been more books on more subjects from more points of view. "Of making many books there is no end," King Solomon observed many centuries ago, and his observations may be truer today than at any other time.

With this in mind I bring myself to the happy task of writing this foreword. Happy because of the extreme importance God places on the subject which this book addresses. I believe the all-consuming purpose of God in this hour of human history is to build His Church, and to build it according to the pattern and plan revealed in His Word.

For centuries, Christians — and church leaders in particular — have largely departed from this pattern and, as as result, the work of God has gone unfinished. "Great" ministries have risen and fallen, the gospel has been preached, and souls have been won; but the overall plan of God has not been fully realized.

Dale Rumble's book has made a significant contribution to the understanding of God's people on the subject of *building the Church.* By carefully presenting the Bible's clear, but much-neglected, revelation on this subject, the author has allowed his manuscript to be lifted well above the category of "just another book" and into the very mainstream of God's great purposes in the earth.

Dale Rumble is a man of integrity and precision, a practical man whose insights have come not merely from intellectual study but from a life of personal action and service. I believe the burden he communicates is the burden of the Lord, and my prayer is that more and more of God's people will be raised up in the days ahead to take hold of that burden, to give themselves — spirit, soul and body — to the completion of God's Master Plan: the building of His Church.

Jim Durkin

Preface

There is no news like good news. The message of spiritual renewal is on the lips of many. The charismatic movement, over the past thirty years, has brought a refreshing experience of new life to the Church. We are living in exciting times, and there is the sound of an abundance of rain in the land. Mercy and grace are being showered upon us from heaven. The Church is being prepared for her Lord's return. Although one cannot hear the sounds of hammers and saws, the house of the Lord is being built throughout the earth.

One of the more significant evidences of this is the widespread interest and growth of home churches or cell groups. The principle of multiplying by dividing is being embraced around the world as a biblical basis for spreading the gospel and reproducing local expressions of the Church. As mainland China opens again, it is apparent that a strong underground church centered around home fellowships has survived. Building the church in homes was the pattern followed by early Christians. One reason is that evangelism, in-depth fellowship, commitment and personal ministry are best developed in small groups. In 1982, a full gospel church in Seoul, South Korea is reported to have had 10,000 home churches, making up a total congregation of over 150,000 believers (this particular church is now much larger). It is breathtaking to consider the potential benefit to the kingdom of God if every church were to adopt this principle!

The challenge for an assembly to take such a step lies in the hands of those holding reigns of leadership, since their stewardship includes the spiritual resources of the church. It may be reassuring for them to know that certain principles work for others, but it requires real faith on their part to lay down conventional methods and put such principles into practice. Many questions will surface: What commitment is required of members? What about our traditions? There are the controversial subjects of shepherding and discipleship. Probably the most important issue to be faced is how to train a numerically and spiritually adequate leadership for home churches. This will raise questions concerning the roles of clergy and laity, of elders and deacons, and of church government.

This book has been written to provide answers for such questions. The text is based on what I have seen the Lord do, both in our local body and in other assemblies, as well as from much research from the Scriptures. I can say that what is presented does work. The contents are presented as an exposition of the following five subject areas. These are written not only for those in full-time ministry, but also for those being trained for the ministry, for elders, deacons and for all who aspire to a place of responsibility in the house of the Lord.

● Why a call to minister is a call to serve.

● Three key disciplines that the Lord brings into the lives of His servants.

● How the local assembly, through the use of home churches and a biblical eldership, can be God's seminary for ministerial training. The relationship of elders, deacons and traveling ministries.

● The order and quality of spiritual life that is being restored to the Church. How the Old Testament tabernacle provides the pattern of what the Lord is doing today among His people.

● How the Lord is preparing His servants for the great harvest and tribulation that will precede His return.

Section One

The Call of the Diakonate

THEME: The Lord Jesus came to earth, not to be served, but to serve and to lay down His life for others. This is the path that each of His ministers is called to walk as well. It is the basis of spiritual leadership. The word *diakonate*, which means "servants," is used to denote *all* who have a place of responsibility in the Church. Those who have spiritual oversight for an assembly are not called primarily to rule the saints, but to love, serve and equip them for service, so that each member can attain the place and ministry he has been called to in the body of Christ. Only in this way will there be sufficient ministry for the Church to mature and function as the Lord intends.

Chapter One

Called to Be Servants

"To Do" or "To Be"?

Where I grew up on the prairies of Western Canada, if you asked young boys what they wanted to become as adults, the chances are their replies would include becoming professional ice hockey players or members of the Royal Canadian Mounted Police. Responses to the same question posed to youths in New York would probably include playing baseball for the Yankees or football with the Giants. Such ambitions arise out of the thrill and glamour of doing great things. It is not too different in the hearts of God's children when they first consider their call in His kingdom. They desire to succeed in ministry, to save the world for Jesus, and to perform great miracles in His name, much of which turns out to be sincere fantasy. It would be quite remarkable if the heartcry of a new believer was: "Lord, help me to be a servant for You."

What does it mean to be called to a ministry, particularly in the growing number of assemblies that recognize spiritual gifts, the five ministries of Ephesians 4:11, and that encourage participation in home churches? How should we prepare ourselves for ministry? What is required of those called into leadership? These are questions that are on the lips of many today, and I will seek to answer them in the pages ahead.

Because of the emphasis and glamour so often associated with the role of public ministry in the Church, I want to establish a fundamental truth at the onset: Greatness is not measured in what *we do for God*; it is based on what we *are in God*. Nothing is greater than becoming a son like Jesus; there is no higher personal goal than seeking to be conformed to His image, and each believer is given this privilege. Not every child of God will become a prophet, an apostle, or an elder; but each one, without exception, is offered sufficient grace and opportunity to be conformed as a son in His image.

The true worth of any ministry arises from the quality of character that has been developed in the one ministering. It is significant that Scriptures dealing with qualities to be found in those called to shepherd His sheep list one qualification four times: the candidate is to be *above reproach*. That is, he is not discredited by his personal life (I Tim. 3:2, 7; Titus 1:6-7). What we *are* in Christ endorses what we *do* in Christ; and what we do is not measured simply in the magnificence of our actions, but by the fruit that is produced as a consequence of them. When the Lord calls a person to a specific ministry, it is not primarily to get something done, for He could have created robots if that was all He had in mind. Neither is the purpose of the ministry to interpret Christ to others. Very simply, ministry is to impart His life, His nature and a knowledge of His ways to others. That precious deposit of Himself within us cannot be imparted to others by simply passing on information, however correct it may be. What we have to offer others will be more readily received if it is *first* demonstrated in our lives; then, instead of preaching "down to them," we present it in an attitude of one who is serving.

Jesus made the Father known to us, not only by His miracles, but by the grace and truth of His life. He came to serve, and out of a willingness to lay down His life as a servant, His ministerial roles as our Shepherd, High Priest and Chief Apostle came to pass. This establishes the pattern for *all* ministry in the Church, and in particular for those called to shepherd the flock of God. They must clearly distinguish in their call between what they are *to be* and what they are *to do*. Elders are not called to be leaders who serve; they are called to servants who lead (by example). In the context of this book the word *diakonate* is not limited to "deacons" but includes all ministers to whom the Lord delegates authority for the work of His House.

> *But Jesus called them* [the disciples] *to Himself, and said "You know that the rulers of the Gentiles lord it over them, and their great men exercise authority over them. It is **not** so among you, but whoever wishes to become great among you shall be your **servant**, and whoever wishes to be first among you shall be your **slave**; just as the Son of Man did not come to be served, **but to serve**, and to give His life a ransom for many."*

Matthew 20:25-28

The Lord calls us by many descriptive names: disciples, friends, brothers, priests, to name a few. If we are truly His disciples, then *first* of all we are His bondslaves. Most of us would accept this as true, but it is also to be the basis of our relationships with one another. Through love we are to serve each other. If we have leadership responsibility, it is easy to believe that we are more important than others. However, if we are humble enough to take a servant's place, we will be less likely to dominate the Lord's people or to compete with our peers and more likely to be a good example to others. Many Christian workers are sincerely committed to serving the Lord, yet in the zeal of ministry they often dominate those entrusted to their care or exercise their ministry in a spirit of competition with others. Zeal to accomplish great things or to be a success can destroy a leader; on the other hand, zeal constrained by the right kind of commitment will endorse him.

Over the years I have often been impressed of my need to pray for a meek and humble spirit. I will continue to do so, for this quality is vital in leadership. It is one reason why God chose Moses. I encourage each one who is called to a place of leadership to test himself by comparing his response with that of Moses when God called him to lead Israel (Ex. 33:12-13).

Moses asked for four things, each of which reflected his meekness of heart:

1. "Let me know *who* You will send with me." He did not trust himself to do it alone, and he sought brothers to help him. This is a picture of collegiality.

2. "Let me know *Thy* ways." Spiritual leadership is based on the ways of the Spirit; Moses knew he was not capable in himself to lead them, for it was beyond his natural ability.

3. "Let me know Thee that I may find favor in *Thy sight*." A leader will only reflect the Lord to His people to the extent that he really knows Him. His objective as a leader must be to please the Lord, not the people; he must not be a "man pleaser."

4. "Remember that they are *Thy people*." The sheep belong to the Lord, not to their overseers. It is discouraging to hear pastors speak of "their sheep." The Lord is their Shepherd, and undershepherds must *never* come between Him and His sheep so as to weaken this relationship. There is danger of this happening in some current practices of shepherding. The emphasis must be on serving, not ruling the sheep.

The Grace of Our Call

It is marvelous when we come to realize that it is utterly impossible within the confines of human resources to fulfill our call. Only God can reveal this to us, but it is something we *must* become assured of if we are to accomplish anything in the kingdom. No matter how much sincere zeal, understanding or ability we can muster, a great gulf exists between what we can do and the fulfillment of our call in God. This gap can *only* be bridged by the grace of God. The Lord will see that we never come into a state at any time in our walk or ministry where we do not need Him. Most of us have some "spiritual scars" from learning this truth.

*Who has saved us, and called us with a holy calling, not according to our works, but according to **His own*** *purpose and grace which was granted us in Christ Jesus from all eternity.*

Second Timothy 1:9

Our call comes from His purpose and is supported by His grace. We are assured of all the necessary resources of His life that we will need to fulfill our call, for He knows what He purposes to do in and through us and lovingly extends the grace we need. It is not a question of how much we need; it is seeing that *all* we require is available. Out of His unlimited fulness we receive grace upon grace upon grace upon grace. We are saved by grace, we stand in grace, we are called by grace, we are taught by grace, and we are enabled by grace.

*I thank my God always concerning you, for the **grace** of God which was given you in Christ Jesus, that in every-thing you were enriched in **Him**, in **all speech**, and **all knowledge** ...so that you are **not** lacking in any gift..."*

First Corinthians 1:4-7

What a picture of supply! Indeed, grace calls into being that which in the natural does not exist. Satan continually points to our needs as reasons why we will fail; God points to them as the reason why we will succeed, for He is our strength.

*And God is able to make **all** grace **abound** to you, that **always** having all **sufficiency** in **everything**, you may have an **abundance** for **every good deed.***

Second Corinthians 9:8

We enter into His rest when our response, faith, efforts and attitudes are in harmony with the principle of grace. It is not that some things are done by the grace of God and other things by ourselves; it is *always* the grace of God working with us. It is vital that our hearts be established in grace; His grace will always prove sufficient for what He calls us to do or to be, regardless of our circumstances. Grace is an expression of His love toward us, and it is *not* to be received in vain. We are laborers *with* Christ. At no time are we excused from the exercise of our own wills, which are never violated by the Lord; He simply knows our weaknesses and provides grace accordingly.

> *But by the grace of God I am what I am, and His grace toward me did not prove vain; but I labored even more than all of them, **yet not I, but the grace of God with me.***

First Corinthians 15:10

Paul frequently referred to his apostolic ministry in his epistles; he did so without self-consciousness or pride, for to him it was purely a matter of God's grace. We can only minister according to the grace given to us, no more and no less. Our lives and our ministry to one another are always to express the grace of God.

> *...Since we have gifts that differ according to the grace given to us, let each exercise them accordingly...*

Romans 12:6

There is *always* more grace available to us than there is sin or inability on our part. If we fail, our victory lies in repentance and seeking grace to help.

> *...where sin increased, grace abounded all the more.*

Romans 5:20

There is more grace extended to the Church than there are needs, and there is more grace available to the world than there is sin.

Grace encourages us when we fail; it points us to Jesus, to His love, repentance and forgiveness. This is why we are exhorted to make sure that *no* one in the assembly comes short of the grace of God (Heb. 12:15). This lack can develop quickly if legalism begins to supplant walking in the Spirit.

We do have a responsibility in receiving the grace we seek. God is opposed to the proud, but He gives grace to the humble. If we believe that we are capable of handling things on our own, we will surely find ourselves short of grace. Also, one does not find grace hidden in the ground or lying in a ditch. It is found *only* at His throne; we are to draw near with confidence to His throne of grace to seek mercy and grace when we have need. Finally, we grow in grace as we grow in our knowledge of Him. The better we know Him, the clearer we see His greatness and the more we see our shortcomings and need of grace. It is not a question of great experiences, but of faithfully coming to Him day by day to receive the grace we need each moment.

I now have a much greater appreciation of the importance of grace in my life than I did as a new believer. In those days my concept of grace was centered largely on myself, in what I was permitted to do within my testimony as a Christian. Today, I see grace within the context of the greatness of God and the bridge of acceptance and supply that He extends to me. I believe we will better appreciate the grace of God once we realize that we are a people called to enter into works which God finished before the world was made. We are an army called to fight battles in a war that is *already won*; we are offered the opportunity to enter into the victory of our Lord from the place of His rest. It is in this context that the sovereignty of God is so important.

Called to Serve His Body

In one of our Lord's titles there is an expression which carries with it a glimpse of our call. By His own will, He has chosen not to be complete apart from Church He purchased with His blood.

> *...And* [God] *gave Him as **head** over all things to the church, which is His body, the **fullness** [completeness] of Him who fills all in all.*
>
> Ephesians 1:22-23

I stated previously that one can have no greater personal goal than to be conformed to His image. However, our destiny is to transcend the goal of individual sonship. The epitome of our call is to fill the place prepared for us in that great completeness of Christ which is His body. Our individual call is sonship; our corporate call is to be built together with other sons so that, as He experientially reigns and lives in each of us, we together constitute a great spiritual man with Him as our Head (Eph. 2:15). This collective relationship is also spoken of in the Scriptures as a "dwelling of God in the Spirit" (Eph. 2:21-22), a "spiritual house" (I Pet. 2:5), and "the city of God, the new Jerusalem" (Rev. 3:12; Rev. 21:2). In our corporate identity, we do not lose our personal responsibility, for we will be judged and rewarded as individuals. However, even this will be in terms of the quality of our integration in the whole body of Christ, i.e. how well has the Lord's prayer of John 17:21-23 been answered by our lives?

It is this relationship with His people that the Lord has purposed to bring forth since the beginning of time. He was not primarily interested in establishing the greatness of Moses, but through Moses He sought to bring Israel forth in the earth as a nation of priests unto Himself. It was not the greatness of Abraham, but the resulting covenant relationship with his seed that the Lord desired. Paul was not called to attain a certain greatness in his apostleship, but to be one whose life and ministry would establish men and women in the body of Christ (Eph. 4:13-16; Col. 1:24-28). All individual calls are oriented toward bringing unto Himself the people whom God has called out of the world. It is within this context of a "plural oneness" in the body of Christ that each of us should view our personal call in God.

We might ask: "Do the Scriptures suggest by what means this fulness will be established?" Obviously, it is a work that *only* the Holy Spirit can do; and did not Jesus say He would build His Church? However, the Scriptures make it clear that He works through spiritually called and spiritually equipped men who *obey* and *serve Him*. Herein lies His call to the *diakonate:* "Be My bond-servants." This is how early Church ministries saw themselves (Phil. 1:1; Col. 4:12; James 1:1; 2 Pet. 1:1). Such men will not seek *primarily* to develop the excellence of their ministry, for their burden is that *each* member of the body of Christ be equipped for service. To this end they will establish converts in accountable covenant relationships where each member can find his place in the life flow of an assembly. All areas of each life must be redeemed: in the home, on the job and in the fellowship. The ideal environment in which this takes place is a local expression of Christ's body under the oversight of servant-leaders who are able to provide the necessary input into lives.

A joint is not a member; it is the interface or "place of relationship" between two members. A healthy body functions, not simply because members are strong, but because their strengths are properly related and coupled to one another. This is the role of joints and ligaments.

*...We are to grow up in all aspects into Him, who is the head, even Christ, from whom the whole body, **being fitted** and held **together by that which every joint supplies**, according to the **proper working** of each **individual** part, **causes the growth of the body** for the building up of itself in love.*

Ephesians 4:15-16

*...Not holding fast to the head, from whom the entire body, being **supplied** and **held together** by the **joints** and **ligaments**, grows with a growth which is from God.*

Colossians 2:19.

Our spiritual growth depends upon the quality of our inter-relationships with brothers and sisters as well as upon our personal relationship with the Lord. Consider the place kicker on a professional football team who trained hard to develop powerful muscles in the hip and calf of his leg, but in the process tore tendons and dislocated his knee. The strength of his leg muscles is then useless to him. His crippled body is no different from a church where a few leaders seek to develop only the excellence of their particular ministries; where people are ministered to, but are *not* brought into the ministry to which they have been called. The unscriptural concept of two classes of saints, namely clergy and laity, has given rise over the years to just such a mentality, and the body of Christ has suffered because of it.

Office or Anointing

During a national election we are visited with endless dialogue and campaign speeches from those seeking public office. It is quite marvelous what is promised at times; and even more marvelous how few promises are eventually carried out. The word "office" carries with it the image of an official and generally impersonal position of responsibility, where the one occupying the office is authorized to perform certain tasks. His ability to do so and to administrate well depends on his being allocated resources in an organization with defined lines of authority.

However, the Lord's Church is an organism. He does not call His servants to fill "offices" in it and He does not build His body through skilled administrators. His resource is the anointing He gives to each member according to his call. This includes responsibility to oversee the lives of others. We are not called to hold offices or to bear titles that carry an implicit authority, but to be brothers serving those entrusted to us with the life of Christ.

> *And do not be called leaders; for One is your Leader, that is Christ. But the greatest one among you shall be your servant.*
>
> Matthew 23:10-11

The word "office" in many churches has come to connote a position or function that, regardless of anointing, has to be filled for a particular function to take place. This is not what is intended where the word "office" has been translated in the Scriptures. When Paul speaks of the office of his apostleship to the Gentiles, the word used is *diakonia*, meaning "ministration" and implies serving (Rom. 11:13). In First Timothy 3:1 the word *episkope* is used in reference to the "office" of overseer. There is no Greek word for "office"; the meaning is simply "oversight" or "superintendence." In both cases, the thought conveyed is that of specific ministry coming forth from a *present* anointing of the Holy Spirit; if there were no anointing there would be no ministry. Equating the call of God with filling an office will lead to a church directed and led by administrators rather than anointed men. Unfortunately, this type of thinking emerged during the initial decline of the early Church, and it has persisted until today. All authority comes from the Lord Jesus Christ and can be delegated by those to whom He has given it, such as the setting of elders in place or the appointment of men to function as deacons. There is *no* authority *invested in an office.* This ceased with the Old Testament priesthood.

While it is incorrect to equate God's call into the ministry with an office, we *are* to recognize the specific *nature* of each ministry given to the Church. To receive a prophet *as a prophet* entitles us to a prophet's reward (Matt. 10:41). There is good reason for the variety God has ordained in His five-faceted love gift of men to the Church. The diversity of His life that is present in the apostolic, prophetic, pastoral, teaching and evangelistic ministries is what ensures the proper building and functioning of His Church. This fivefold class of ministries is often referred to as "ascension gift ministries" (Eph. 4:10-11). It is to ensure this supply of His life to equip the saints that the Lord calls forth elderships made up of such men.

I am sure all of us at times have had problems in knowing how to properly honor those whose ministry has blessed us while still giving the glory to God. We don't want to exalt the man and cause him to be lifted up in pride, but we do want to show our appreciation of him. No doubt we have all fallen into the trap of comparing one ministry with another, which is displeasing to the Lord. There is a proper way to view the Lord's ministers without having these problems. Three things are involved in *valid* ministry: the vessel who brings the ministry, the ministry itself, and the grace of God that provides the ministry. We are to relate to each of these as follows:

● **Love** *the vessel;* this is always true regardless of how good or ineffective the ministry may be.

● **Receive** *the ministry;* since God has sent it, we are to recognize the ministry for what it is and receive it. We don't receive an apostle as "just another preacher."

● **Honor** *the grace of God;* a great ministry means great grace, and we honor the Lord accordingly by recognizing this. We are *never to exalt the vessel or the ministry (Gal. 2:9).* When we follow these simple rules we will maintain proper priorities in our heart attitudes toward those who minister to us.

His Universal Call

What are we to see as the ultimate objective and consummation of our call in God? What is the vision we are to impart to those whom we disciple? I submit that the following are the most frequent responses one would receive if all born-again Christians were asked this question:

● to win as many souls as possible for the Lord.

● to know the Scriptures thoroughly and to be able to teach and impart this knowledge to others so that they would know how to live godly lives.

● to bring concepts of the kingdom of God into society, and so remove all social wants and injustices.

● to be a person of faith, such as those listed in Hebrews Chapter 11.

● to minister with signs and wonders so that the sick are

supernaturally healed, demons are cast out and the works of Satan are destroyed in the earth.

● to be completely successful in ministry (i.e., as a pastor, teacher, etc.).

Although these are fine objectives, none fully expresses the vision God has for us. Even when combined they fall short.

I remember my own experience in this area of understanding what I was called to do and how it related to the purpose of God. In 1953, hands were laid on me and I was prophetically called to be a teacher. As my wife can testify, I immediately set about to do this. She saw me only when I occasionally surfaced from behind my Bible and a pile of books. I prayed for open doors, and neglecting my family when opportunities came, I would go and teach. I focused on becoming the best teacher I knew how; that was my vision. Thirteen years later, this word of the Lord came to me: *"The mouth of a teacher, but from this day forth the heart of a shepherd."* My vision was enlarged, and (belatedly) I became more involved in the lives of those whom I was teaching. In the years that followed, God began to establish in my heart certain practical implications of the concepts I had been teaching. Much theory became translated into reality. I learned many new things, most of them simple. I saw how God's love used differences in His children as sandpaper to deal with unpleasant personality traits and to bring secret things into the light. He made me conscious of the need to remove facades and to be honest in all areas of my life with those with whom I fellowshipped. As iron sharpens iron, so we began to sharpen one another in deeper dimensions of fellowship. Through these things God spoke new understanding into me concerning my ministry in building His Church. In a greater measure I began to see His purpose in my life, my family and the body of Christ. I am sure that most Christians are not as dense as I was; nevertheless it is God who must reveal such things to us, and this will occur only as our hearts are stretched and prepared for it.

The Lord certainly desires that the lost be redeemed, as well as all of the other stated objectives; but what is the greatest desire of His heart? Is it not that *He* be glorified in His people, glorified in the Church He has purchased with His own blood, in those with whom He will complete His ministry in this age and who will be presented to Him as a bride without spot or blemish? Is it not to build for Himself out of living stones a habitation of the Spirit where He will rest for eternity; a city set on a hill that cannot be hid because it is filled with His glory? I believe it is so! When we lump together all valid ministries along with all He has commanded us to be and do, we discover His final objective: He is coming back to be glorified in His saints! (2 Thess. 1:10) I cannot be content only with my life being in order, although that will glorify Him; I am to serve so as to bring forth His glory in others. This is the heart of our call.

The Wisdom of Our Call

Everything the Lord does has its beginning in His wisdom—not a wisdom of reaction to the unexpected when things go wrong, but the wisdom of divine strategy based on His foreknowledge of all things. My inheritance and call in God were established before the world was made. This is clearly shown to us in Proverbs eight where wisdom speaks to us in the first person confirming these things. Listen to her words:

The Lord possessed me [wisdom] *at the beginning of His way, **before** His works of old. From everlasting I was established, from the beginning, from the earliest times of the earth. When there were no depths I was brought forth, when there were no springs abounding with water. **Before** the mountains were settled, before the hills I was brought forth; while He had not yet made the earth and the fields, nor the first dust of the world. When He established the heavens, I was there, when He inscribed a circle on the* *face of the deep, when He made firm the skies above, when the springs of the deep became fixed, when He set for the sea its boundary, so that the water should not transgress His command, when He marked out the foundations of the earth; then I was beside Him, as a master workman; and I was daily His delight, rejoicing always before Him, rejoicing in the world, His earth, **and having My delight in the sons of men**.*

Proverbs 8:22-31

The wonder of it! Divine wisdom rejoicing in all that was planned for the life of each of His children centuries *before* they were born. How dare we believe the Lord doesn't know or care what is happening to us? He did not predetermine what we must do, but, foreknowing our free-will decisions, He brings into our lives those things that encourage us to make the correct choices so as to glorify Him and to fulfill our call.

My life is not ordered by chance. I am sure all of us have encountered times of trial in our lives when we didn't know what to do or where to turn. When we sought Him with all our hearts, in time we saw that our circumstances were an ordered pattern of events woven by the Lord for our good. These were intended to build understanding and character in our lives as we went through them. For example, the testing of our faith can produce steadfastness (James 1:3). Once we are completely committed to the will of God, we can have great peace by recognizing that the flow of our life only encounters whatever events the wisdom of God has ordained for our good and His glory. *All* things work together for the good, *if* we love God and are called according to His purpose (Rom. 8:28).

Our existence in this life occupies but a small dot on the scale of time in which the Lord moves. In the beginning, at minus infinity if you will, the Lord in His wisdom planned all that He would do. *Nothing* has transpired since then by satan or man that was not foreknown by Him. We are not to regret or dwell on those things we might have done better before we were saved: "I wish I had gone to college"; "If only I had followed my parents' advice"; "If only I had married someone more spiritual." The Lord knew what it would take for us to respond to His call, and where we find ourselves fits perfectly into that call. We are to understand that there are reasons why we were born at this time and not under the Old Covenant or in the first generation of the Church. The wisdom of God planned our call in His purposes for *today*. And it is important that we never allow needs around us to replace the purpose of God as our goal in ministry.

We are to see our life span as a tiny instant in time, during which we have the privilege of entering into the great stream of events that has been occurring over the centuries. All of history is destined in the end to contribute toward the consummation of His eternal purpose among men; this purpose is hidden in Scriptures and has our call and destiny woven into it (Is. 46:9-10; Ps. 33:11-12). It is concealed only that it might be revealed to those who will seek it out (Mark 4:21-23).

> ...*That the God of our Lord Jesus Christ, the Father of glory, may give to you a spirit of wisdom and of revelation in the knowledge of Him. I pray that the eyes of your heart may be enlightened, so that you may know what is the hope of His calling, what are the riches of the glory of His inheritance in the saints.*

> Ephesians 1:17-18

Because He *foreknew* what the free-will response on our part would be to His call, He made provision to justify us and then extended the richness of His grace to enable and help us through every circumstance of our lives. If He is so committed to our success, who can really hinder us? The discipline He brings into our lives, our obedience and prayers, all work together to prepare us for His glory. It is quite marvelous to realize that the Scriptures speak of these things in the *past* tense, that is, as having been *already* accomplished. In Romans eight we read that those whom He *foreknew* He *predestined* to be conformed to the image of His Son; therefore He has *called* them, *justified* and *glorified* them (verses 29 and 30). We need only work out that which has already been completed in Christ; by entering into work that is already finished, we enter into His rest. No wonder it is known as a holy calling!

Section Two

Discipled by God

THEME: The Lord seeks to do a deep work in the hearts of those who represent Him in feeding and caring for His people. One cannot build spiritual truth into the lives of others until it first is present in his own life. It is one thing to have our sins forgiven, to be filled with the Spirit and know the Scriptures; it is quite another to be able to say: "Follow me as I follow Christ." Those who lead others are to lead by example, and particularly in righteousness.

*Remember those who led you, who spoke the word of God to you; and **considering the result of their conduct, imitate their faith**.*

Hebrews 13:7

There are three key areas in lives of leaders where the Lord brings His discipline to bear in order to manifest His character:

- righteousness in their personal lives.
- faithfulness in their commitment to Him.
- purity in their speech.

Chapter Two

Discipled to Righteousness

The Touch of the Master

The oil paintings by great masters reflect characteristics and qualities of their creators; people who know art can look at such works and easily identify the artist who painted them. It is the same with disciples of Christ. Implicit in all biblical discipline is the fact that a true disciple is one who is taught and trained by the Lord and therefore exhibits the qualities and handiwork of his Master. We are to manifest the intrinsic qualities of His character in our lives and our relationships together so as to reveal Him to the world; what a challenge this is!

> *A pupil* [disciple] *is not above his teacher, but everyone, after he has been fully trained, will be like his teacher.*
>
> Luke 6:40

It is recorded that the Apostle John discipled Polycarp, and that the character of Christ which was so rich in John could also be seen in Polycarp. The secret was that John had *first* become like his Teacher. If we preach the gospel of the kingdom, we are responsible to obey it so we can honestly say: "Follow me as you see I follow Christ."

The focus of ministry to new converts is first to bring them into a solid personal relationship with Christ through experiencing the work of His cross. The horizontal relationship and ministry they will have to others later will in the end be based on the foundation of their vertical relationship to Christ. Righteousness is what sets us apart from all other people.

Too often believers assume that after having their sins forgiven and being baptized in the Holy Spirit, they will naturally walk in victory over sin; they soon find this isn't so. There has been a failure to appropriate all that was provided at Calvary. Too often, this comes from not understanding the significance of water baptism in relationship to a victorious walk. Let us see what the New Testament has to say concerning this important foundational truth.

Water Baptism in the Gospels

The era of the New Testament began very dramatically. After a period of many years without a word from God, suddenly out of the desert there was heard the loud, clear voice of a prophet proclaiming the ways of the Lord. It was John the Baptist calling the sons of Israel to repentance. He focused on the state of their hearts; in essence he said, "Repent and get right with God." His message of repentance is the first step of redemption and was the basis for all New Testament ministry. Only if their heart attitude was right could the children of Israel receive the person and ministry of their Messiah. John came to prepare His way, proclaiming the new, unfolding covenant relationship God would establish with men through His Son.

The word John preached had three major elements of truth:

1. He pointed people to Jesus as the sacrificial Lamb of God to take away their sin.

...Behold, the Lamb of God who takes away the sin of the world.

John 1:29

2. He made it clear that in order for Israel to receive the Messiah it was necessary to truly repent of all sins. Those who did repent John baptized in water.

...The word of God came to John, the son of Zacharias, in the wilderness. And he came into all the district around

the Jordan, preaching a baptism of repentance for the forgiveness of sins.

Luke 3:2-3

3. John promised that the One coming after him was much greater than himself, and He would baptize with the Holy Spirit all those who repented and turned to Him.

As for me, I baptize you with water for repentance, but He who is coming after me is mightier than I, and I am not fit to remove His sandals; He will baptize you with the Holy Spirit and fire.

Matthew 3:11

The three truths of his message dealt with blood, water and spirit.

When Jesus began His ministry, the first step He took was to show His support of John, being baptized by him in the Jordan (Matt. 3:13-15). In this way He provided a continuity between John's ministry and His own. Throughout the time that He preached, those who received His words were also baptized.

When therefore the Lord knew that the Pharisees had heard that Jesus was making and baptizing more disciples than John (although Jesus Himself was not baptizing, but His disciples were)...

John 4:1-2

After the Lord's death and resurrection, He manifested Himself to the disciples, instructing and commissioning them to be His witnesses, and this instruction included water baptism.

*Go therefore and **make disciples** of all the nations, **baptizing** them in [into] the name of the Father and the Son and the Holy Spirit, **teaching** them to observe all that I commanded you.*

Matthew 28:19-20

The Early Church Practice of Baptism

Once we appreciate the emphasis placed on water baptism in the gospel era, we should examine the practice of baptism by the early Church, for this provides the pattern for Christian baptism today. The Church was born on the day of Pentecost in the promised outpouring of the Holy Spirit. Many of those present were greatly convicted of their sins. When these people asked what they should do, the Apostle Peter charged them as follows:

Repent, and let each of you be baptized in the name of Jesus Christ for the forgiveness of your sins; and you shall receive the gift of the Holy Spirit.

Acts 2:38

It is remarkable how similar these words of Peter were to those of John. Some three thousand responded and were baptized that day. We should be clear that the centrality of the gospel was *always* Jesus Christ and *not* baptism or any other sacrament.

And every day, in the temple and from house to house, they kept right on teaching and preaching Jesus as the Christ.

Acts 5:42

Water baptism became immediately important only when people responded to the message of grace, repented of their sins and turned to Christ as their Savior. This is evident in the record of Philip's evangelism at Samaria.

And Philip went down to the city of Samaria and began proclaiming Christ to them. ...But when they believed Philip preaching the good news about the kingdom of God and the name of Jesus Christ, they were being baptized, men and women alike.

Acts 8:5,12

Philip did not bring the people to a saving knowledge of Christ and then put them on probation to see if they were truly saved before baptizing them. On the contrary, as soon as they confessed Christ they were instructed and baptized *immediately.*

An excellent example of the importance of water baptism is found in the story of the Ethiopian eunuch. This particular man had gone to Jerusalem to worship. He was now returning home, hungry in his heart to know the ways of God. Although there had been disciples in Jerusalem, the Lord did not use them to lead him to Christ (possibly to instruct us better through the record of Philip's ministry). The Lord directed Philip to leave Samaria and go to a desert road leading from Jerusalem to Gaza. He arrived at the eunuch's chariot to find him reading Isaiah 53. This is a wonderful Scripture, often called the "Gospel of the Old Testament," since it deals prophetically with the Lord's sacrificial death. The eunuch asked Philip for help in understanding the contents. Philip opened his mouth, and beginning at Isaiah he preached Christ to him. It might appear there was no reason to mention baptism, for there is no record of baptism in Isaiah and little likelihood of finding water in the desert. Nevertheless, as Philip preached, the eunuch interrupted him and said:

> *...Look! Water! What prevents me from being baptized?*
> Acts 8:36

Upon his confession of faith in Jesus Christ, it is recorded that he and Philip went down into the water and he was baptized. Although the message preached by Philip centered on the vicarious death of Jesus, it must also have included the command to be baptized in water. Philip did not neglect teaching on baptism just because circumstances were not convenient for a baptismal service.

The first Gentiles to receive the grace of God did so under Peter's ministry to the household of Cornelius. When God gave these Gentiles the Holy Spirit, it must have been a traumatic experience for the Jewish believers present. They began to realize that God's covenant was being extended beyond the borders of Judaism to include the uncircumcised. The proper theological position would suggest they had better pray first, discuss it, and research the Scriptures before accepting what God had done. However, Peter immediately focused their attention on one thing:

> *"Surely no one can refuse the water for these to be baptized who have received the Holy Spirit just as we did, can he?" And he* **ordered** *them to be baptized in the name of Jesus Christ...*

Acts 10:47-48

Water baptism was not presented as an option; it was given as a *command!*

Another example of the early Church practice in baptism is found in the ministry of Paul and Silas to a jailer at Philippi. Because they preached the gospel, Paul and Silas had been beaten and put in jail with their feet in chains. At midnight, while they were praying and worshiping the Lord, an earthquake opened the doors and loosed their chains. The jailer was about to kill himself, since he faced death if the prisoners escaped. When he realized that Paul and Silas were still present, he changed from a man who was about to take his life to one seeking eternal life. His question to Paul and Silas was the best he could have asked:

> *Sirs, what must I do to be saved?*

The answer was not: "Be baptized," and you will be saved, but...

> *Believe in the Lord Jesus, and you shall be saved...*

Acts 16:31

That same hour the word of the Lord was preached to the jailer and his household. We are not told how many believed, but *all* who did believe were baptized that night, possibly only an hour or two after midnight. There was no thought of a probation period, church membership, consideration of the jailer's religious tradition or anything else; baptism was presented as an *immediate* act of faith that was to accompany repentance and faith in Christ.

Rebaptism

Frequently I encounter Christians who question whether they should be rebaptized. Some are adults who were baptized as infants and are seeking to reaffirm what they believe took place then. There are others who previously had been baptized as adults but did so without true repentance and conversion. Still others are not at peace because they had such a limited understanding at the time they were baptized. There is a scriptural basis for rebaptism. Paul discovered some believers at Ephesus who had followed John the Baptist and were baptized by him. However, there had been no follow-up ministry to them. They apparently were not familiar with the death, burial and resurrection of Jesus and certainly had not heard of the coming of the Holy Spirit. In other words, their first baptism had been based on promises of what was yet to happen and not to appropriate what had occurred at Calvary. Paul's instruction brought these disciples of John into a commitment to Christ.

> *"John baptized with the baptism of repentance, telling the people to believe in Him who was coming after him, that is, in Jesus." And when they heard this, they were baptized in the name of the Lord Jesus.*
>
> Acts 19:4-5

It is not necessary to make a great issue of rebaptism; I believe that when sincere Christians receive sound teaching on the subject, the Holy Spirit will convict those who need to be rebaptized.

The Name

It was the same Holy Spirit in Jesus who also anointed Peter to speak as recorded in Acts 2:38. For this reason, Peter's command and the early Church practice of baptizing in the name of the Lord Jesus Christ could not be at variance with the Lord's command in Matthew 28. They are the same. This can be seen by considering His name.

To be baptized into "the name of the Father, and the Son and the Holy Spirit" means just that; we are baptized into *one* name that is representative of the Godhead. "Father" is a title, not a name; the same is true for "Son" and "Holy Spirit." The key is found in the name of Jesus. "Jesus" (which is *Joshua* in Hebrew) literally means "Johovah saves." Thus Jesus possessed the name of His Father.

> *...And I come to Thee. Holy Father, keep them in **Thy** name, the name which Thou hast given Me, that they may be one, even as We are.*
>
> John 17:11

Through the Spirit, all the fulness of deity dwelt in Him and He is called by the name *Christ,* or the "Anointed One." He was the only human, visible manifestation of the Holy Spirit (Col. 2:9).

Thus the name "the Lord Jesus Christ" does represent the Godhead with all representative authority given to Him (Matt. 28:18). For this reason, His name is used by the Church as authority for *all* actions, not just water baptism.

> *And whatever you do in word or deed, do all in the name of the Lord Jesus...*
>
> Colossians 3:17

The Significance of Baptism

The gospels and the Bood of Acts provide a clear picture of the practice of water baptism. However, it is the epistles that explain *why* it is important. Salvation is based on the following fundamental truths:

1. Christ died for our sins.
2. He was buried.
3. He arose from the dead through the power of the Holy Spirit.

> *For I delivered to you as of first importance what I also received, that Christ **died** for our sins according to the Scriptures, and that He was **buried**, and that He was **raised** on the third day according to the Scriptures.*

First Corinthians 15:3-4

Jesus died with a mortal body, one such as ours (although without sin). His body was buried in the tomb, where it remained for three days. When the Spirit of God raised Him from the dead, Jesus did not simply regain natural life in a mortal body. Instead, He arose in an immortal body, one with eternal life. He came out of the grave with a new, glorified body; one that, although it still bore the marks of the crucifixion, was different. Mary did not recognize Him, nor did the disciples on the road to Emmaus.

Jesus willingly shed His blood in death on the cross so that whoever repents and receives Him is saved. When this happens, they are forgiven all sin and stand innocent before God. It is His blood that covers all transgressions and sins, cleanses our consciences and sets us free from the penalty of sin. However, God desires more for us than the forgiveness of our sins. He wants to change us so that we do not continue in sin but are conformed to His image. More happened at Calvary than the shedding of His blood to forgive sins. When Christ died, our old nature was also crucified with Him.

> *Knowing this, that our old self **was** crucified with Him, that our body of sin might be done away with, that we should no longer be slaves to sin; for he who has died is freed from sin.*

Romans 6:6-7

For this reason, we are to identify with His death by the "burial of our old nature," that just as Christ arose in a new body, we too can come out of a grave of water no longer under the domination of sin. This step, after the forgiveness of our sins, requires the exercise of our faith in those Scriptures that speak of putting off the old nature through baptism.

> *Therefore we have been **buried with Him** through baptism into death, in order that as Christ was raised from the dead through the glory of the Father, so we too might walk in **newness of life**.*

Romans 6:4

In this context, baptism certainly means immersion, for we would never just sprinkle soil on a dead body to bury it. The place for faith is great concerning our walk after baptism; just as I believe that His blood cleansed my sins, I must also believe that I am now dead to old habit patterns of sin and can walk in righteousness because He now lives His life in me through the Holy Spirit.

> *Even so consider yourselves to be dead to sin, but alive to God in Christ Jesus.*

Romans 6:11

I have baptized a number of believers who, although truly saved for a period of time, seemingly could not give up some sin or bad habit (such as smoking). Through water baptism with instruction, I have seen those hindrances disappear from their lives.

> *I have been crucified with Christ; and it is no longer I who live, but Christ lives in me; and the life which I now life in the flesh I live by faith in the Son of God, who loved me, and delivered Himself up for me.*

Galatians 2:20

By faith I see myself as having been crucified with Christ two thousand years ago. Although physically I could not have been there on the cross, one thing I can do now is to identify with Him in the likeness of His death through burial. By this act, I testify that I *have been* crucified with Him and am now putting my old carnal nature into a grave of water, out of which by the power of the Spirit I will arise to walk in newness of life. This body of truth is so *often* the neglected key for those who do not have victory in their walk.

*...In the cross of our Lord Jesus Christ, through which the world **has been** crucified to me, and I to the world.*
Galatians 6:14

Christ was raised from the dead by the power of the Spirit; we also need the indwelling Holy Spirit if others are to see His resurrection life within us.

The Threefold Witness

In order to appropriate fully the death, burial and resurrection of Jesus, we must identify our commitment to Him by faith in His blood, the waters of baptism and the Holy Spirit. These were the three salient points of focus in John the Baptist's message, in the Lord's work of atonement, and in the ministry of evangelism by the early Church.

*For there are **three** that bear witness, the **Spirit** and the **water** and the **blood**; and the three are in agreement.*
First John 5:8

An excellent picture of this threefold witness of our salvation is pictured in God's deliverance of Israel out of Egyptian bondage (Ex. 14). Egypt is a type of sin and the world, out of which we have been called into fellowship with Christ. The first step in the children of Israel's deliverance was their obedience in placing some blood from the Passover lamb upon the door posts of their homes. By this act they escaped the judgment of God's death angel. This foreshadowed the death of Jesus as our Passover Lamb.

The next step was their exodus from Egypt. As the nation of Israel departed, they were pursued by their Egyptian tormentors and taskmasters. The Lord directed His people to go into the Red Sea which, by His power, opened for them to pass through but then closed and destroyed their enemies.

This is a picture of water baptism, which takes away those enemies in our life that had kept us in the bondage of sin!

The third step relates to Israel's guidance by the pillar of fire and cloud through the Red Sea toward the Promised Land. God's presence in the cloud provided guidance to His people. This speaks to us of His presence with us and the personal leading of His Spirit in our lives. Exodus, therefore, presents a picture of blood, water and Spirit in redemption.

The Covenant Seal

The key that links water baptism with the Abrahamic covenant is found in the book of Colossians. The following quotation is taken from the Amplified Version:

> *In Him also you were **circumcised** with a circumcision not made with hands, but in **spiritual circumcision** performed by Christ by **stripping off** the body of the flesh the whole corrupt, carnal nature with its passion and lusts. Thus you were circumcised when you **were buried with Him in your baptism**, in which you were also raised with Him to a new life through your faith in the working of God as displayed when He raised Him up from the dead.*

Colossians 2:11-12

Every born-again Christian is a child of Abraham, the father of *all* the faithful. Abraham believed the promises of God made to him, and on the basis of his faith righteousness was imputed to him. Through faith God established His covenant with Abraham. While the covenant of the law of Moses, introduced four hundred and thirty years later, was fulfilled at Calvary, this covenant of faith has *never* been set aside (Gal. 3:17-18). We enter into the promises of this covenant through Christ, who was the true promised seed of Abraham and in whom the promises are fulfilled. We, like Abraham, do so on the basis of faith. The promises were made to Abraham and to his seed (singular), which is Christ, and by faith through Him to us. The New Testament is the fulfillment of the Abrahamic covenant (Gal. 3:16).

After Abraham believed, God required that he take upon himself a seal, or sign, of the covenant that they had entered into. He and all male Israelites were to be circumcised. This was the seal. Since the covenant continues in effect today, so also should the seal.

> *And he received the **sign of circumcision**, a seal of righteousness of the faith which he had while uncircumcised, that he might be the father of all who believe without being circumcised, that righteousness might be reckoned to them.*

> Romans 4:11

Heart circumcision is the New Testament seal of covenant relationship with Almighty God. The seal given to Abraham provided cleanliness to the physical body and was a type or shadow of the spiritual cleanliness we are to possess. It is important to see that Abraham had righteousness imputed to him by faith *before* he was circumcised. Likewise, we believe in Christ and receive His imputed righteousness before we are baptized. We are a covenant people and the sign of our covenant is to be in our walk of righteousness.

> *But he is a Jew who is one inwardly; and circumcision is that which is of the heart, by the Spirit...*

> Romans 2:29

The seal of our covenant is not the act of immersion, but the spiritual circumcision that takes place within us at baptism.

There are many sincere Christians who seek for victory in their walks through various ways and beliefs. Some emphasize an experience of sanctification, others look for deliverance from evil spirits, still others attempt to live under legalism, following strict rules of conduct. The true key for victory is our faith and appropriation of what Christ *has already accomplished* for us on Calvary. This is what the Lord seeks to establish early in the life of each disciple, and especially in those who lead.

Chapter Three

The Discipline of Commitments

Covenant Commitment

Matthew is our house cat. He is committed to our home because he gets fed and has a warm place to stay. However, he is aloof and belongs to no one. Jackson, the family dog, belongs to my son and is totally obedient to him. He too is committed to our home, but he is also submitted to someone. He gives as well as receives.

It is one thing to be committed to the family of God just to receive the benefits. It is quite another thing to be also personally committed to serving others. Covenant commitment is a two-way street. When we are first converted, there is generally a great deal of enthusiasm but not too much practical understanding of how we are to commit ourselves or what is required of us. We have a warm feeling knowing that we belong to Him. However, there is little comprehension of the battles that lie ahead wherein we learn the principles of submission and obedience.

The word "covenant" is defined in dictionaries as a "formal, binding agreement." It is not an agreement based on casual assent; it is a *binding* commitment between the parties concerned. The heart of both Old and New Testament theology is the covenant God initiated with Abraham on the basis of his faith in believing specific promises made to him by the Lord. The covenant was entered into by the Lord with the redemptive purpose of calling a people out from the world for Himself; a nation established in righteousness that would be salt and light in the earth, and that would minister to Him as a kingdom of priests. Everything hinged on the strength and perpetuity of this covenant. It took approximately thirty-seven years for the Lord to establish the covenant with Abraham and test it through the offering up of Isaac.

There were three distinct steps of commitment required of Abraham. The first step required him to leave his family and country and go to a land he did not know. If he would do so, the Lord promised to bring forth a nation from his seed and to bless the earth through it (Gen. 12:1-3). In other words, he first had to be *willing* to lay aside the natural relationships of his family and country for the sake of a promised commitment to the Lord by faith. As a result of his obedience, God imputed righteousness to him. These acts of commitment made by Abraham are steps that we as His covenant people must also take. Let us consider the first step and what it means to us.

Committing Ourselves to Christ

We often do not appreciate the singular commitment that is implicit in the covenant we have entered into with the Lord. For this reason, instead of forsaking other allegiances, we mingle them with our commitment to Him and thereby weaken it. There are three areas in particular where this mixture is most common:

1. *FAMILY.* We are clearly directed to raise and establish our children in a covenant relationship with Christ. Much of what the Lord has been doing in recent years is reestablishing proper family order in families. The Spirit has been turning the hearts of fathers to their children and hearts of children to their fathers (Mal. 4:6). However, when relatives and family members choose not to follow Christ, we *cannot* put our relationship with them above our covenant with the Lord. Jesus made this clear in His teaching:

> *Do you suppose that I come to grant peace on earth? I tell you, no, but rather division; for from now on five*

members in one household will be divided, three against two, and two against three. They will be divided, father against son, and son against father; mother against daughter, and daughter against mother; mother-in-law against daughter-in-law, and daughter-in-law against mother-in-law.

Luke 12:51-53

He who loves father or mother more than Me is not worthy of Me....

Matthew 10:37

2. *COUNTRY.* Nationalism and patriotism are not pertinent to our covenant with Christ. It is proper to pray for our country's leaders and to thank God for a land where we have religious freedom. However, America and democracy have nothing to do with the kingdom of God. If we walk in the righteousness of our covenant with God, we will bless the land we inhabit and be as the goodness of salt in it. Nevertheless, our citizenship and allegiance are centered in heaven. Our commitment to Him should never be diluted by support of any political cause. Our help will come from Him alone. It is He who raises up and removes kings.

3. *RELIGIOUS AND SOCIAL CAUSES.* There are many good causes to which we can give ourselves. However, if this service does not flow out of covenant relationship to Christ and is not an extension of church life, we would be well advised to lay it down. Many Christians are totally committed to supporting social causes without realizing that the *only complete* answer for all problems is the bringing in of His kingdom. When the work of the para-church groups involved in preaching the gospel is oriented toward building sectarian kingdoms which promote competition and disunity in the body of Christ, they become a contradiction of the ultimate intent of His covenant. Allegiance to such groups should be avoided. We have been bought with a price, and we belong *totally* to Him. All we are and have is His; in return, all He has is ours. We

are to have an undivided heart in our covenant with Christ. Too many Christians are committed to a church to serve Christ rather than committed to Christ to serve the Church.

Many times I have heard ministers point to the relationship of David and Jonathan as a good example of covenant commitment. Yet nothing is farther from the truth. It is one of the saddest examples of family relationship taking priority over commitment to a godly covenant that can be found. It was not a lack of true love, for Jonathan loved David even as himself. He protected him from his father's anger, for he knew that David was the Lord's anointed and would one day take over the throne of Israel. He twice covenanted with David in his zeal of commitment. He spoke covenant. He meant it, *but he never walked it out!* It doesn't add to a covenant to write it out and sign it; all that counts is keeping it. When David fled with other outcasts to the cave of Adullam, Jonathan never left the comfort of his father's house to accompany him. The sad final end of their relationship came when Saul died on the battlefield and Jonathan died with him. Would David have committed those sins that later marred his reign as king if he had his friend Jonathan to sit beside him and provide input into his life? Jonathan's love and commitment to him was the *one thing* God knew he would need as king.

The same failure was also true for Michal, the daughter of Saul, who married David. She loved him and also protected him from death at her father's hand. However, she too never left home to be with David in exile. Because she was not with him, she came to have spite in her heart for him. As a result, their marriage was never blessed with children and she died barren. Jonathan's death and Michal's barrenness were the consequences of failing to walk out a covenant with the Lord's anointed simply because they did not value it above their parental relationships.

Commitment is a two-way street; as we commit ourselves to Him, He, in turn, commits His treasures to us; and He does so to the degree that we have committed ourselves to Him. For example, at the first level of commitment we do not have much understanding; we know it is Jesus who has saved us and we have committed our souls into His hands. He is our Savior. In turn, He commits to us a responsibility to proclaim the gospel we have embraced. This first level of commitment is portrayed in the following two Scriptures:

> *...But I am not ashamed; for I know whom I have believed and I am convinced that He is able to guard what I have **entrusted** to Him until* [for] *that day.*
>
> Second Timothy 1:12

> *Now all these things are from God, who reconciled us to Himself through Christ, and gave us the ministry of reconciliation, namely, that God was in Christ reconciling the world to Himself, not counting their trespasses against them, and He has **committed** to us the word of reconciliation.*
>
> Second Corinthians 5:18-19

To all who commit their lives and souls into His hands, the Lord commits the word of reconciliation. They receive a ministry commensurate with what they have committed to Him. They have received eternal life, and they are to persuade others to entrust their souls into the hands of the Savior. In essence they are able to minister out of what they have become in God: one of His children. It is unfortunate that many Christians spend their entire lives knowing only this level of commitment.

Committing Our Ways to Christ

The story of Abraham illustrates how important the second level of commitment was in his life. Although he had righteousness imputed to him on the basis of faith, yet his personal life was not all it should have been. In Egypt he lied to Pharaoh concerning his wife. This was done out of fear, very much as a coward would act. Later he was unable to see how God's promise of a son could be fulfilled because of Sarah's advanced age. As a consequence he went in to Sarah's maid, Hagar, that she might give him a son; and Ishmael was born as a result. We all face the same problem if we seek to bring forth ministry by our own ability. Unfortunately, it often takes a long time for us to realize that the best we can offer of our ways will accomplish nothing in the kingdom of God. There is no supernatural endowment of human efforts. The second level of commitment is faced on our part, when we can honestly admit that our ways are *not* His ways, and we are willing to lay them down and yield ourselves totally to Him. Consider Paul's challenge to do this as he addressed the believers in Rome:

*I urge you therefore, brethren, by the mercies of God, to **present** your bodies a living and holy sacrifice, acceptable to God, which is your spiritual service of worship. And do not be conformed to this world, but be transformed by the renewing of your mind, that you may prove what the will of God is, that which is good and acceptable and perfect.*

Romans 12:1-2

When we commit our own righteousness, our human ability, our personal preferences, our committees, our techniques and clever ways of thinking into His hands, realizing the best we can do will never be accepted by the Lord, then we are in a position to be given His ability. It is out of our personal weakness that He entrusts us with His power. It is only by time spent in His presence for prayer and worship that we truly appreciate the reality of our personal weaknesses.

...Most gladly, therefore, I will rather boast about my weaknesses, that the power of Christ may dwell in me.

Second Corinthians 12:9

...And to him who lacks might He increases power.
Isaiah 40:29

The Lord chooses for Himself those who are seen as foolish, weak and despised in order to put to shame what is viewed as great by the world. When we commit our ways to Him, He in turn entrusts to us the riches of an anointed ministry for the sphere of service to which we have been called. He begins to live within us in new dimensions. We commit the weakness of our human ways to Him; He entrusts His ministry of the Spirit to us. This is how we enter into His rest.

*For the one who has entered **His** rest has himself also rested from his works...*
Hebrew 4:10

Again, this level of commitment is a two-way street, for He commits Himself to us in the same measure to which we lay down our ways.

Abraham entered into this second, deeper phase of commitment when God required him to take upon himself a seal of their covenant relationship through the act of circumcision (Gen. 17:9-11; Rom. 4:10-16). This act required Abraham to shed some of his blood. In fact, what he did was to "cut covenant." Circumcision signified physical cleanliness. In turn, the Lord later ratified (or cut) the covenant on His part by coming to earth and shedding His blood on the cross. His blood provides the spiritual cleanliness by which we walk in newness of life after we have buried our old nature through the circumcision of Christ in the waters of baptism. After Abraham was circumcised, a new righteousness became apparent in him. This is seen in his intercession for Lot in Sodom and in his willingness to offer up Isaac as a sacrifice.

Committing Ourselves to Serve

It is in the third level of commitment that we realize the full fruit of our covenant relationship with Christ. The consummation of Abraham's covenant was not in the birth of

Isaac; it came a number of years later. The Lord waited until Abraham's love deepened for the youth while he grew into early adolescence. Then God tested Abraham by asking him to sacrifice Isaac. There was not the slightest hesitation or questioning on Abraham's part. He immediately departed with all that was necessary, and he did not take an alternative offering. When he raised his arm to slay the boy, the Lord stopped him, for Abraham had proved he did indeed understand that all he possessed belonged to God. He valued the covenant to God more than the promise of the covenant. In God's eyes, this was the final step of their covenant commitment.

This is the place of testing where many charismatic Christians are today. In recent years the spiritual gifts, ministries and graces of the Lord have been poured out. Now, He is asking us to offer them up to Him in service. We are *not* to build our kingdoms with them or to major on the excellence of our ministries. For our commitment to be complete with the Lord, we are to offer up what we have been given in the Spirit to serve His people. An effective *DIAKONATE* can only come out of a commitment to *serve* those for whom their ministry is intended. Ministry is not an impersonal act, it is life flowing out of a heart's compassion and love toward others. Paul expresses his commitment to those he reached out to in his apostolic ministry with these words.

> *...I have a stewardship **entrusted to me** [the second level]...For though I am free from all men, I have made myself **a slave** to all [the third level], that I might win the more. And to the Jews I became as a Jew...To the weak I became weak...I have become all things to all men, that I may by all means save some.*
>
> First Corinthians 9:17-22

Again, Paul, speaking for himself, Silvanus and Timothy, expressed it this way to the Corinthian saints:

> *For we do not preach ourselves but Christ Jesus as Lord, and ourselves as your bond-servants for Jesus' sake.*
>
> Second Corinthians 4:5

This third level of commitment is a fundamental and necessary step for all who are of the *diakonate.* Spiritual ministry without an attitude of serving will accomplish little. Shepherding will be superficial when it does not come from the heart of servants. One of the best practical examples of serving to be found in the Scriptures is seen in the record of Jesus' crucifixion. Despite His agony on the cross, Jesus did not forget the physical care His mother would require after He was gone.

> *...He said to the disciple, "Behold, your mother!" And from that hour the disciple took her into his own household.*
>
> John 19:27

As in the other two levels, this is also a two-way street. We discover that if we commit ourselves to serve others, they will respond and commit themselves to us; love demands a response. The giving and responsive love of bonded brothers is what holds a church together; we are called to be a brotherhood of God's sons who are constrained by His love to walk together in an unbreakable covenant. Once we are committed to maintaining this union to one another in the love of Jesus, then neither satan nor problems can divide us. It is the practical demonstration of this love and unity between members of the body of Christ that is light in the world. It is vital for assemblies to walk in this level of covenant if their members are to grow up in Christ and fulfill their ministry. The Church is an organism of life, not an organization held together with doctrinal agreements and membership roles.

Commitment to His Word

Finally, one cannot speak of being committed to the Lord without being eagerly committed to His Word. It was

Abraham's faith in the Word of God that undergirded his covenant relationship, and the Lord places the same emphasis on all who are in covenant with Him.

And as for Me, this is My covenant with them, says the Lord. My Spirit which is upon you, and My words which I have put in your mouth, shall not depart from your mouth, nor from the mouth of your offspring, nor from the mouth of your offspring's offspring, says the Lord, from now on and forever.

Isaiah 59:21

The only unchanging things in this changing world are God and His Word (Ps. 119:89). In the glorious and perilous times ahead I believe the Lord's work in the Church will bring us a much greater appreciation of just how precious and certain His Word really is. It is a manual of discipline that never needs updating. If we are to enter into our full inheritance and return to Him the fruit He seeks in our lives, we must be doers as well as hearers of the word. Truth is not a passive knowledge of what is correct; it arises out of the dynamics of doing what is correct. It is good to remember that the ultimate objective of the Lord's ministry to the Church is to cleanse her through the washing of water with the Word, that He might present her to Himself in all her glory, a sanctified people without spot, wrinkle or any such thing.

I have endeavored to demonstrate the importance of the Word of God through a liberal use of the Scriptures as authority for the various points I make in the text.

It is one thing to know the Scripture; it is another thing to be able to present the Word so that it brings life to others. Let us consider how the Lord trains us to speak for Him.

Chapter Four

Discipled to Speak

The most difficult member of the body for each of us to rule is our tongue. James says if one can do so, he is able to control his entire body (James 3:2). It is not enough to know what to say; we must also speak with a spirit that does not hinder our words. If we speak truth but do so with a bitter spirit, our words can bring death to the hearer even though they are absolutely correct. We are exhorted to keep our heart with all diligence, for out of it are the issues of life; and this issue is primarily through our words. Anyone can talk about the Lord, but not everyone can speak for Him. The area of speech, therefore, is a vital area of discipline for all who are called into the *DIAKONATE*.

We are not able by our own strength alone to achieve victory. We read Scriptures such as the following and find that no matter how hard we try, we are unable to obey them consistently:

> *...there must be no filthiness and silly talk, or coarse jesting, which are not fitting, but rather giving of thanks.*
>
> Ephesians 5:4

> *Therefore, laying aside falsehood, speak truth...Let no unwholesome word proceed from your mouth...Let all bitterness and wrath and anger and clamor and slander be put away from you...*
>
> Ephesians 4:25-31

It looks hopeless, and we agree with brother James:

> *But no one can tame the tongue; it is a restless evil and*

*full of deadly poison. With it we bless our Lord and Father;
and with it we curse men, who have been made in the
likeness of God.*

James 3:8-9

We need to be bridled by the Lord. This was the heartcry
of David in one of his prayers:

*Set a guard, O Lord, over my mouth; keep watch over
the door of my lips.*

Psalm 141:3

How does the Lord do this wonderful work?

The Bridle Phase

There are four redemptive steps in this phase. First, we
must clearly see our need. We are to see ourselves as Isaiah
did with respect to the holiness of God:

*..."Woe is me, for I am ruined! Because I am a man of
unclean lips, and I live among a people of unclean lips;
for my eyes have seen the King, the Lord of Hosts." Then
one of the seraphim flew to me, with a burning coal in his
hand which he had taken from the altar with tongs. And
he touched my mouth with it and said, "Behold, this has
touched your lips; and your iniquity is taken away, and
your sin is forgiven."*

Isaiah 6:5-7

God must sovereignly reveal His glory and His holiness to
us. When this happens we too will say: "Woe is me, for I am
a man of unclean lips." The fire of the Holy Spirit touches
our hearts and shows us the enormity of our need and our hopeless
position apart from His purifying power. We cannot represent
a holy God unless we put aside the unholy traits of wrath,
malice, slander, and abusive speech from our mouths. We
must lay aside falsehood and speak truth to each other, for
we are members of one another. Thus, first of all in the bridle
phase we become conscious of the great need we have in the

area of our speech habits, and we turn to the power of the Holy Spirit to help meet that need.

Secondly, the Lord teaches us that we must begin to rule our spirits. If indeed my words express what is in my heart, then I must first rule there if I am to control my words. The Lord will bring practical dealings into my life to show me where and why I lack control and how I can make Him Lord in these areas of my life.

> *Like a city that is broken into and without walls is a man who has no control over his spirit.*
>
> Proverbs 25:28

The third aspect of the bridle phase occurs when God begins to reveal the value of silence. There are many instances and circumstances when we should be silent. These provide opportunities for us to practice ruling our spirits. For example, when Herod had Jesus brought to him for questioning, Jesus did not answer him. There are times also when we should not speak what is precious to us, such as when it would mean nothing to the hearer.

> *Do not give what is holy to dogs, and do not throw your pearls before swine...*
>
> Matthew 7:6

There are many Christians with preacher's itch who would speak anytime to anyone. A true witness knows when to speak and when not to speak. A prompting for silence comes from the Lord just as much as a prompting to witness. We are called to be witnesses of Christ, not just speakers of words!

An instance calling for silence is found in the story of the woman who was caught in the act of adultery and taken before Jesus by her accusers. There had been witnesses of her act, and the law said that under this condition she was to be stoned. Jesus was bound to keep the law, but He also wished to minister mercy to the woman. He did not know what to speak; therefore, He stooped down and in silence waited for His Father to give Him a word of wisdom. We too must learn to be swift to hear and slow to speak. When we do not know what to say, silence is always correct. It is written:

> *He who guards his mouth and his tongue, guards his soul from troubles.*
>
> Proverbs 21:23

Also, silence is a golden reaction when we are enveloped in unpleasant circumstances that God has brought into our lives. Since these are for our good, He wants us to learn by going through them without complaining. It is written of Jesus:

> *He was oppressed and He was afflicted, yet He did not open His mouth; like a lamb that is led to slaughter, and like a sheep that is silent before its shearers, so He did not open His mouth.*
>
> Isaiah 53:7

Further examples of the value of silence are those times when we are tempted to make decisions based only on our emotions. When the Lord was transfigured before His three disciples, Peter said:

> ..."Master, it is good for us to be here; and let us make three tabernacles: one for You, and one for Moses, and one for Elijah" — not realizing what he was saying.
>
> Luke 9:33

What Peter said was neither pertinent nor profitable. Emotions are never a good basis for making spiritual decisions.

Silence is also beneficial whenever God uses our conduct to speak to someone. This is pointed out in Peter's exhortation to wives:

> ...*You wives, be submissive to your own husbands so that even if any of them are disobedient to the word, they*

may be won without a word by the behavior of their wives.

First Peter 3:1

Many times what we are and what we do speak louder than anything we could say. God knows when an unbeliever will not listen but will observe. A well-timed silence can say more than speech.

Other circumstances that call for silence include maintaining the privacy of counseling and times when it is better not to speak of certain things that we may happen to know concerning someone.

It is the glory of God to conceal a matter...

Proverbs 25:2

In the course of building relationships, counseling and sharing lives together, we often acquire understanding of events that should not be made public. If we are trustworthy we will not reveal them. The love of God will cover and conceal as well as expose. If we speak when we should remain silent, we can never be sure where our words will eventually go, nor what harm they will do.

Furthermore, in your bedchamber do not curse a king, and in your sleeping rooms do not curse a rich man, for a bird of the heavens will carry the sound, and the winged creature will make the matter known.

Ecclesiastes 10:20

What seems to be a harmless word that we do not expect to be heard will often resound through the church and eventually hurt someone.

Probably the most important time to be silent is when we come into the presence of God and He would speak to us.

There will be silence before Thee, and praise in Zion, O God...

Psalm 65:1

Time spent in prayer and silence before the Lord is the basis of being able to speak for Him.

> *The Lord God has given Me the tongue of disciples, that I may know how to sustain the weary one with a word. He awakens me morning by morning, He awakens my ear to listen as a disciple.*
>
> Isaiah 50:4

How many times when someone is sharing a problem with us do we begin to answer with the Scriptures before we completely understand the problem? This is not right. God has given us "hearing ears" as well as "seeing eyes" so we may know how to answer.

The fourth and final objective of the bridle phase is to discipline our choice of words when we do speak. To this end, our Father's exhortation may sound something like this paraphrase of Ecclesiastes 5:1-2:

> *All right now, My son, you can speak; but remember that where there are many words, transgression is unavoidable, and he who restrains his lips is wise. Also guard your steps when you go to My house, and draw near to listen rather than to offer the sacrifice of fools. When you speak, do not be hasty in word or impulsive in thought to bring up a matter in My presence. Let your words be few so that you do not let your speech cause you to sin.*

This diminishes our *self-confidence;* we are no longer sure we have all the answers. We learn to say, "If the Lord wills, I shall do this, and I shall say that." We begin to speak words out of His life rather than from our knowledge about Him.

The fast of God described in Isaiah chapter 58 deals with those things one must lay aside to have the glory and blessings of the Lord upon his ministry. This includes, in part, ceasing "to speak our own words" (v.13). The world says "talk is cheap"; God says "mere talk leads only to poverty" (Prov. 14:23). Empty words are not cheap; they are destructive and costly. When we look at a horse after it has been tamed, we recognize by its bridle that it has been mastered; also, as we exhibit a bridle on our mouths, do we show proof that God owns us. It is the most important piece in the harness of relationship that we wear in the body of Christ!

Do all things without grumbling or disputing; that you **may prove** *yourselves to be blameless and innocent, children of God above reproach...*

Philippians 2:14-15

Our sonship and character are validated by an absence of grumblings and disputings. This is a fruit of the bridle phase.

The Life Phase

After we have experienced the bridle, there begins an enrichment of life in our words. When we prepare to minister, we are now more concerned with our heart than with our knowledge. We are impressed with the need for quiet times in worship and prayer, since there must be sweet water in the pipeline if we are going to water the garden of the Lord. When our hearts are filled with good things, they can be released as life. However, for this release to become a flow of life, it must be governed by an anointing of the Holy Spirit. It requires the wisdom of God to impart spiritual knowledge through words so that it is received as life by the hearers. Such wisdom is not primarily related to the mechanics of speech but to the purity of our spirits when we speak. It is the fragrance of His nature carried by our spirits that makes our words acceptable. What we are becomes the basis of how and what we speak.

The tongue of the wise makes knowledge acceptable...

Proverbs 15:2

The wise in heart will be called discerning, and sweet-ness of speech increases persuasiveness.

Proverbs 16:21

The heart of the wise teaches his mouth, and adds persuasiveness to his lips. Pleasant words are a honeycomb, sweet to the soul and healing to the bones.

Proverbs 16:23-24

The Apostle Paul puts it this way:

Let your speech always be with grace, seasoned, as it were, with salt, so that you may know how you should respond to each person.

Colossians 4:6

With His wisdom we can speak to the spiritual, the carnal or the lost, and minister life in each case. If our heart attitude is divorced from the words we speak, all we will accomplish is to pass on information and concepts. The Lord tells us to feed His sheep. He did not instruct us to give them information from our minds, but to feed them from our hearts.

Peacemaking is a ministry of relationship where the words spoken and the character of the one speaking must both express peace to be effective. A brother offended is hard to be won, and only a ministry of peace in the Spirit of God can bring reconciliation between such parties. A peacemaker is a person whose words bring the Lord's government into the lives of those in disagreement. Wherever Christ reigns, His government and peace are present. Making peace is not deciding who is right, but bringing Christ into His rightful place in each situation. When both parties are reconciled to being under the Lordship of Christ they will be at peace with one another. An apology is the best way to have the last word!

Christ cleanses the Church by the washing of water with His Word. I do not bring cleansing by pronouncing Scriptures of judgment, but by speaking an appropriate word in love. It is the word received and obeyed that cleanses. Love is patient and kind. It will not brag nor act arrogantly; it will bear all things, believe all things, hope all things, endure and cover those things that need to be put away. However, the love of

God also speaks the truth in confrontation. If we have been through the bridle phase, we are able to speak truth to others because our heart attitude has been dealt with. Once God has delivered us from a harsh, biting, cutting spirit, He can trust us to use His sword. The Word of God is sharp; used skillfully, it is the means of speaking truth in love, of separating soul and spirit, and exposing the carnal nature as well as satan's kingdom. It is to be used as a surgeon's knife, not a woodsman's axe.

The flow of words and life in body ministry pictured for us in the following Scripture can be the experience of every local assembly:

> *...Put on a heart of compassion, kindness, humility, gentleness and patience; bearing with one another, and forgiving each other, whoever has a complaint against anyone; just as the Lord forgave you, so also should you. And beyond all these things put on love, which is the perfect bond of unity. And let the peace of Christ rule in your hearts, to which indeed you were called in one body; and be thankful. Let the word of Christ richly dwell within you, with all wisdom teaching and admonishing one another with psalms and hymns and spiritual songs, singing with thankfulness in your hearts to God.*
>
> Colossians 3:12-16

Jesus spoke as one having authority. Spiritual authority will generally be recognized and received by others when it is seen coming from a godly character. Paul exhorted Timothy to speak, exhort and reprove with all authority, and his counsel to Timothy addressed what was needed for him to be accepted in his role as a young leader.

> *Let no one look down on your youthfulness, but rather in speech, conduct, love, faith and purity, show yourself an example of those who believe.*
>
> First Timothy 4:12

Leaders are to conduct themselves so that the grace and gentleness of Christ's nature endorse the words they speak. This is particularly true in their relationships with one another, for if leaders cannot flow as one, they will never lead the flock into unity. Some time ago, at a local shepherd's conference, the Lord prophetically called us to lay down our swords and daggers. We were told not to use doctrine or tradition to cut or stab one another. The Scriptures state that the Lord's bond-servant must not be quarrelsome. Christ does not need us to argue His case, nor should we defend our own. How often we wound others in the cause of what we think to be correct!

We are to minister in faith: We must never excuse the word He gives us, we must not apologize for it, we need not justify it, we dare not add to it, and we must not exaggerate it. We are simply to speak what He gives us. In addition, we must be careful not to dissipate the anointing with too many words, even when we have a clear message from Him. We should be like Elijah who spoke words that God stood behind. Elijah prayed that it would not rain, and it did not. Elijah said that fire would come down, and God sent the fire. We need to be men whose words are both given and confirmed by the Lord. Life can only flow out of the anointing of God. Words of life must be His words and be expressed in a spirit that prepares the hearts of the hearers to receive them. In this way His words can be spirit and life to serve His people.

Let the words of my mouth and the meditation of my heart be acceptable in Thy sight, O Lord...

Psalm 19:14

Summary

In the last three chapters we have considered three very important areas of personal training where we are discipled as sons to bring us into a strong vertical relationship with our Father. If this training is unfruitful, then we cannot expect success in training others, for disciples will be like their teachers. The objectives of this discipline can be summarized as follows:

● To attain a walk in righteousness so that we are an example to those who follow us. We are not to live under the dominion of sin.

● To be totally committed to the covenant relationship we have entered into with Christ and His people. It is a common mistake of many to assume they are committed to Christ just because they are heavily involved in working for Him. Involvement is not the same as commitment. When you eat ham and eggs for breakfast, the chicken was involved in your meal, but the pig was committed to it. Commitment requires some death on our part.

● When we possess redeemed speech, our words will not cause us to sin or offend others, but will endorse our ministry. There are, of course, many other areas where the Lord's discipline touches our lives, but these three should be evident in the lives of those who build His house.

Section Three

God's Seminary, the Local Assembly

THEME: My first experience in building a church began three years after my conversion. My wife and I gathered people together in various homes in the community for mid-week Bible studies. Later, we found an abandoned schoolhouse in the countryside. We fixed it up, bought a used organ and began bringing in children for Sunday school. In time adults and children gathered together for Sunday meeting. My primary emphasis was a "full gospel" message supported by a great deal of teaching. I had built my first church, or so I thought. Three years after we began, in a very sovereign way, the Lord called us to the Hudson Valley region of New York State. A brother came in to take over the work. It was not many months before the church had vanished. I had built nothing! In reality, everything had depended on me. I taught the people, but I did not equip them. In particular, I had not trained men for responsibility. The next two chapters deal with the things I did not do.

It is evident that assemblies during the period of the early Church were under the oversight of a plural eldership. Since there were no Bible schools as we know them in those days, one may ask, "How were these men trained, and how can we follow such a pattern today?" The answer is that more than education is required; it involves a "grass roots" discipling of candidates by practical applications of the Word across all areas of their personal lives. The objective is to produce men who are committed to serving the Lord and His people from a place of responsibility. A local assembly structured around a format of home churches and teaching is an ideal seminary. Here, a wholesome balance of practical and spiritual life qualities can be developed. The syllabus is instruction plus a daily working out of what is taught through on-the-job training. The faculty is a college of men related together in spiritual oversight of the assembly and home churches. The emphasis is not on how to rule others, but on how to *serve* them.

The heart desire of Christ is that every member of His body be equipped for service. It is the responsibility of those ministries who plant, build and oversee churches to ensure that this equipping takes place. For this reason, my emphasis is focused more on these directive ministries than on the other equally valid spheres of service in the body of Christ.

Chapter Five

Deacons, Elders and Traveling Ministries

A Seedbed

The root definition of *seminary* comes from "semen" (seed) and means "seedbed or nursery." *Webster's New Collegiate Dictionary* defines it as "an environment in which something originates and from which it is propagated." This describes precisely what local assemblies are to be in God's economy. First of all, they are bodies of believers who, having been properly established by the Holy Spirit upon the Lord Jesus Christ as their foundation, constitute corporate local expressions of His life. Secondly, they are environments from which spiritual ministries are raised up and released to give birth to further expressions of His body. Everything in the earth to which God has given life goes through a cycle in the course of its propagation. If the life cycle is interfered with, it is possible to retard or eliminate a species. While not as obvious a principle, this is equally true for the Church.

The Lord Jesus, in addition to His ministry to the multitudes, trained disciples to build His Church. After Pentecost, they were sent out from Jerusalem to evangelize and establish converts together in viable local expressions of His body. The church at Antioch was birthed by disciples who were scattered from Jerusalem because of persecution; Barnabas and Paul were then led there by the Lord to build these converts together into a body (Acts 11: 19-26). In a similar fashion, Philip was chosen to birth the assembly at Samaria, while Peter and John provided subsequent foundational ministry for these believers (Acts 8). Apostolic teams, were sent out from Antioch to plant churches in a number of cities (Acts 13:1-3).

These examples all represent the initial phase of church life. Unless the first assemblies produced ministries which were capable of raising up new assemblies, there would be no growth of the Church sufficient to evangelize the world. The seed life would soon die out, and the commission to preach the gospel to all men would be abdicated. It is not a question of imparting authority to act from one generation to the next, but is a matter of the continued reproduction of spiritual life in men. It is one thing to say, "I give you the same authority to minister that the Lord gave Peter or Paul"; it is quite another to impart the life and ministry Peter or Paul had. Only the fiber of His life can constitute a true basis for the life cycle and quality of the Church. Ministries of the second and third generation after Pentecost failed to sustain the vision and excellence of the first disciples, and consequently what they built was also lacking. Thus began cycles of decline that fed upon themselves until the apostasy of the Dark Ages was realized. A spiritual organism of life capable of reproducing itself was replaced by organizational directives. The many-membered body of Christ ceased to be a functioning body and became two distinct groups of individuals: clergy and laity. However, it is out of the depths of failure that revival comes. Where sin and failure abound, grace abounds even more. In recent years, God has been graciously restoring our hearts to His purpose for the Church. We are no longer living in a time of declension but in one of ascension, a time of building up His Church that she might embrace the purpose to which she has been called.

Servants

To appreciate what is pertinent to the life cycle of an assembly, it is necessary to evaluate what the Scriptures teach about the training and interrelationship of deacons, elders and traveling ministries. There has been much light shed in recent years on the ministry of elders as well as on traveling ministries. However, very little has been written on the relationship between these ministries and elders or between elders and deacons.

The first thing to recognize is that only the Lord can build his Church. He alone knows the pattern; He chooses the workers, and He equips them for their ministry. We only need look at the diverse structures of churches in Christendom to recognize that what man has tried to organize into being can only grow out of the life of Christ.

On the subject of serving, when all is said and done, more is said than done. A spiritual principle that must be imparted as a heart attitude to those chosen for training in ministry and oversight is that they are called to be servants who lead rather than leaders who serve. The priority must be what they are rather than what they do. The first disciples are often referred to in the Scriptures by the Greek word *doulos*, meaning "slave" or "bond-servant". The word *diakoneo* means "to wait on, to serve or minister to." I have chosen to use the word *diakonate* to denote all who serve from a place of responsibility in the church, including deaconnesses, older sisters who teach younger sisters, deacons, elders and the five ascension-gift ministeries of Ephesians 4:11. I have done so in order to bring a needed focus on this principle, which is basic to the spiritual life of a church. Anyone called to give direction to others can follow no better example than that set by Jesus:

> *For who is greater, the one who reclines at the table, or the one who serves? Is it not the one who reclines at the table? But I am among you as **the one who serves**.*
>
> Luke 22:27

The Corporate Diakonate

Paul's epistle to Philippi was addressed both to the saints and to the elders and deacons who cared for them. Elders and deacons together are a "corporate *diakonate*" for an assembly since they jointly serve the flock. I have often heard it said, "Deacons are to serve, but elders are to rule." We need to settle it on our hearts that all ministry functions, all those in leadership in a church, are servants. Elders and deacons are to be united as one in the commitment to serve the Lord and the flock. The mantle of leadership does rest upon the elders. However, both are servants, and if serving is not the basis of leadership, the tendency will be for elders to lord it over the flock. This results in a man-directed church, which was Peter's concern in his exhortation to elders:

> *...I exhort the elders among you...shepherd the flock of God among you, exercising oversight not under compulsion, but voluntarily.... **nor yet as lording** it over those allotted to your charge, but proving to be **examples** to the flock.*
>
> First Peter 5: 1-3

What better example of eldership can be set for a church than a group of godly men who in love and humility serve with the responsibility for oversight shared equally; men who are committed to standing together through all circumstances with one mind in overseeing the flock of God? This does not imply that all have the same grace in ministry, the same visibility or the same stature in God. Some who are seen less in public ministry from the pulpit can be deeply involved in the lives of those needing counsel and personal care. Where some may be visible through a teaching or prophetic ministry, others are burdened with the daily cares of shepherding. A biblical elder must have one of the ministry graces of Ephesians 4:11. Because of this diversity, great trust and confidence must be present among those in the *diakonate*. It was Paul's concern that this kind of bond be established between the elders at Ephesus to protect the church. He didn't warn them about satan, but he was greatly concerned about their heart attitudes toward one another.

> *Be on guard for yourselves and for all the flock, among which the Holy Spirit has made you overseers, to shepherd the church of God...I know...savage wolves will come in among you, not sparing the flock; and from among your own selves men will arise, speaking perverse things, to draw away the disciples after them.*
>
> Acts 20:28-30

I am surprised by the number of times I have met men committed to building local expressions of the body who are uncertain of the role of deacons. Deacons are intended to provide a vital functional undergirding for the elders; without deacons there can only be a weak and limited eldership. When local churches are formed without deacons, elders must handle many tasks and functions that sap their time and strength away from what they are anointed to do. As the church grows and greater demands exist for teaching and counseling, many of the "lesser tasks" are assigned to men appointed as "elders who are less capable in the Word and Spirit." These men become de-facto deacons. Although they have the title of elders, they lack the grace of a biblical elder to equip and oversee believers.

Eventually, the need for proper order becomes necessary when it is apparent that the existing leadership is not adequate to bring forth the life and growth that should characterize the body of Christ. There will be concerns of how to train disciples and raise up new men into eldership while still handling all the daily problems that arise. At this time a distinction must be made between the elder-deacon functions. When men have been set in place as elders to perform these supporting tasks and they lack the anointing to oversee, to equip and feed the flock, both the elder and the deacon roles will be weakened. It is at best unpleasant to "unappoint" an elder, but this must be done when an improper foundation has been laid. Eventually, there should be a greater number of deacons supporting the eldership than there are functioning elders.

Titles should be avoided until the anointing and fruit for an emerging ministry is evident to all. If a title seems necessary before an appointment can be made, "responsible brother" is always appropriate. The key is His life. A local church is a valid expression of Christ's body only if His life is visibly present in both the character and ministry of the people. As a new assembly grows, in time some members will manifest this life in roles of serving through what is clearly a God-given ability to shepherd and equip others. These are the elders, and in time they will be recognized as such by all who see their need for shepherding, even before they are set in place.

Elders

The task of shepherding a church was never assigned to one person in the New Testament. It was always committed to elders, a group of men who, although diverse in ministry, were equal in sharing governmental responsibility (Acts 14:23; Acts 20:17; Titus 1:5; 1 Pet. 5:1-2). The Greek word for elder, *episkopos*, can be translated as "overseer," "elder" or "bishop."

Some will say that a plural collegial leadership will not work; however, experience proves otherwise. If one in the eldership believes himself to be greater than the others, then indeed there will be problems. Heart-bonds of mutual trust and love must exist between them. This kind of union does not occur overnight but is developed by walking through difficulties and stresses faced together in real-life situations.

From my own experience in an assembly at Kingston, NY, where I first embraced this truth, I can testify that the stress was very real. This was particularly true in my relationship with one brother. My peers could testify equally so in their relationship to me, especially since I was older and more set in my ways. The fruit came when, by God's grace, we realized the bond between us was strong in the love of Christ and would *not* be broken. The pastoral relationship I now experience with the men with whom I am yoked in eldership is one of the most important things in my life. The stress we experienced was necessary to develop the trust and confidence we now have in one another. The lack of such a relationship was the primary concern Paul had for the elders at Ephesus (Acts 20:30).

Elders have two basic areas of responsibility:

1. To minister the Word of God (i.e., to feed and equip the saints).

> *An overseer* [elder], *then, must be...able to teach...*
> First Timothy 3:2

> *For the overseer must be above reproach as God's steward...holding fast the faithful word which is in accordance with the teaching, that he may be able both to exhort in sound doctrine and to refute those who contradict.*
> Titus 1:7-9

2. To exercise the authority inherent in overseeing and guiding the church.

> *Obey your leaders, and submit to them; for they keep watch over your souls, as those who will give an account...*
> Hebrew 13:17

> *But we request of you, brethren, that you appreciate those who diligently labor among you, and have charge over you in the Lord and give you instruction.*
> First Thessalonians. 5:12

We *cannot* delegate our ministry to another person, for it is derived from the anointing and grace that rests upon us. Authority, on the other hand, *can* be delegated. All authority is held by Christ; whoever He entrusts with authority may in turn delegate it to others. Elders are responsible to exercise their particular ministries in the Word and Spirit. However, authority for the oversight and management of certain church affairs can be delegated by elders to responsible men and women. It is not a question of shirking responsibility, but one of maintaining proper priorities between shepherding functions. This includes the discipling and training of new ministries. We tend to think only of the time required for counseling and preaching, but much time must also be spent by the elders, first with one another, and then with those who are being trained. This is not possible if they are also heavily engaged in administration or related supporting functions.

I believe that the training and equipping (or discipling) of men for the *diakonate* is probably the most neglected and needed ministry in churches today. The dual structure of leadership makes each local assembly a literal Bible school, or seminary, for the raising up of ministries in the body of Christ. Those undergoing training for leadership should have authority delegated to them for limited spheres of responsibility to develop and test their faithfulness and fruitfulness. Philip, who was one of the seven men selected to serve as a deacon in Jerusalem, later became a successful evangelist, due in large part to his earlier faithfulness in serving others.

The training process for potential elders is not simply one of teaching them how to minister, but also of establishing the godly character necessary to endorse their ministries. Qualifications for elders focus more on personal righteousness and home life than on ability in ministry. One of the great merits of plurality is the mutual protection afforded against deception and error, because each person's life and character is open to the correction and admonishment of his peers on a daily or weekly basis. Therefore, training will involve learning how to share one's life with others and being open to correction. Some of the character traits listed in the Scriptures for elders are the following:

...must be above reproach, the husband of one wife, temperate, prudent, respectable, hospitable, not addicted to wine, not pugnacious, gentle, uncontentious, free from the love of money, able to manage his own household, possessing a good reputation outside the church, not accused of dissipation or rebellion, not self-willed, not quick-tempered, loving what is good, sensible, just, devout, self-controlled.

First Timothy 3:2-7; Titus 1:5-9

Integrity is not formed by just listening to good teaching; it involves the dynamics of putting teaching into practice, making mistakes, being corrected, going through the dealings of God and learning from example. It is important that those undergoing training be occasionally given opportunity to sit with the elders in their meetings and travel with them as they minister. The life of Christ in a person is as much the basis for discipling others by being seen in day-to-day conduct as in preaching. We can impart no more to others than we possess of Him ourselves. The best gift we can give others is a good example.

Good insight into what the Lord requires of shepherds is found in His admonition through Ezekiel to the shepherds of Israel. This is a valid prophetic word for the Church today.

*...Woe, shepherds of Israel who have been feeding themselves! Should not the shepherds feed the flock? You eat the fat and clothe yourselves with the wool, you slaughter the fat sheep without feeding the flock. Those who are sickly you have not strengthened, the diseased you have not healed, the broken you have not bound up, the scattered you have not brought back, nor have you sought for the lost; **but with force and severity you have dominated them.** And they were scattered for lack of a shepherd...*

Ezekiel 34:2-5

An attitude of dominance and "lording it over others" is the antithesis of laying down your life for those entrusted to your charge. Such an attitude has historically been a major hindrance to the testimony of the Church. This attitude is spoken to in the above chapter where the Lord lists His complaints against those responsible for tending His people. He repeatedly points to it as the key reason why His sheep have become sickly and scattered. In verse 4, He condemns shepherds who rule the sheep with force and severity rather than feeding and caring for them. In addition, He speaks out against fat sheep who dominate weaker ones in the flock. They had become like the shepherds over them. It is not just leaders who can hinder the spirit of love and unity in the assembly; *all* can be guilty who believe their spiritual stature is greater than others and seek to be recognized for it. This is why it is so important that elders set a proper example in humility for others in the flock to follow. What the elders are is what the sheep will become.

> *Therefore, thus says the Lord God to them, "Behold, I, even I, will judge between the fat sheep and the lean sheep. Because you push with side and with shoulder, and thrust at all the weak with your horns, until you have scattered them abroad..."*
>
> Ezekiel 34:20-21

In verse 17, the Lord promises to judge between one sheep and another and between the rams and male goats. While I am not exactly sure who in the flock of God male goats and rams refer to, I am certain they are not the meek and lowly of spirit. They are not those who strengthen and encourage the weak and sickly, nor are they concerned for those who have come short of the grace of God and thereby developed a root of bitterness. They certainly do *not* have hearts given to shepherding and caring for others.

> *Is it too slight a thing for you that you should feed in the good pasture, that you must tread down with your feet the rest of your pastures? Or that you should drink of*

> *the clear waters, that you must foul the rest with your feet? And as for My flock, they must eat what you tread down with your feet, and they must drink what you foul with your feet.*

Ezekiel 34:18-19

These verses speak of an environment where there has been no example of true shepherding demonstrated before the sheep.

From the *diakonate* in many local assemblies over the land the Lord is raising up shepherds today who are bond-servants after His heart, men who will seek out His sheep and gather them together in His house where they can be fed, equipped and cared for.

Priorities

Each local church is birthed from His life and grows and reproduces through His life. Therefore, the problem is not finding the "right structure" of elders and deacons in order to preserve His life in the assembly. It is to recognize that His life *alone* can sustain the church and produce scriptural order. Our priority must be *Him*, not the structure. While the *diakonate* is responsible to function within a scriptural order of relationship, it must serve in such a manner that Christ is *always* kept central in the people's eyes. For example, good teaching, if those teaching are not watchful, can replace the people's need to seek the Lord daily in the Scriptures for themselves; the same holds true for counseling. This dependency on a strong ministry *must* be avoided. When Christ occupies His rightful place as Shepherd and Head in the hearts and priorities of each member, then His blessings and glory will be abundant in the church. This reflects the order of His life; where He is Lord, there is order!

It was in this area several years ago that the Lord severely dealt with those of us who were elders in our assembly. As is so often the case, we were unaware there was a problem. We thought that as a church we "had arrived." There was good worship and good life flow in body ministry. There was a good number of home churches, apostolic and prophetic ministries were emerging, and there were excellent shepherding, teaching and counseling ministries. What could be wrong?

The Lord spoke to a young man in the assembly and gave him a prophecy to read in church. The message began like this: "You say you have built Me a strong house; I say you have built a tent, and I am going to cut the ropes of that tent. ..." That was *exactly* what He did, and I was the first rope! He did not shake the church, but He certainly adjusted the leadership. The problem was profound, but one that could easily be overlooked when there is too much emphasis on structure and order rather than on the Lord Himself.

The problem was that our ministries had become too central in the lives of the saints. Instead of seeking the Lord in His Word, the people were being fed by the teaching ministry. When there were personal problems, those with problems would come for counsel from the elders instead of first going to the Lord. In short, the elders were *coming between* the Lord and His people. He was not being seen as the Shepherd, Counselor and Teacher of the Church. We were ministering to needs more than bringing each one into the relationship with the Lord where He would meet their needs. There was too much emphasis on the horizontal dimension of ministry! The Lord insists on being head over *all* things in the life of each believer. This is what order is all about. How did He cut the ropes? He brought circumstances into my family life that greatly reduced the time I could spend in ministry. He also dealt with the other elders. Once we understood the problem we began to exhort each believer to personally seek the Lord in greater measure.

Without going into details, I can say that the eldership was shaken and tested in a number of ways. In addition, some in the flock who had leaned too much on elders encountered problems that only the Lord could handle in a sovereign way, which He did. Body life today in the church surpasses what we had known before. We still have a long way to go, but by His grace we are learning how much He loves us.

There are four essential areas of commitment for those in an eldership:

1. To keep Christ in His rightful place as Lord and Shepherd of the flock.

2. To stand as one man, being accountable to one another in serving and overseeing the flock.

3. To support and honor one another.

4. To recognize the unique ministry each one has.

I believe these four areas of commitment are listed in their correct order of priority; unfortunately, the fourth one is often given far too great an emphasis. When this is the case, the virtues and value of collegiality can be greatly weakened. One with a strong, more visible ministry has a greater responsibility to be an example to the others in humility and show a willingness to take the lowly place among them. To do so will *strengthen*, not weaken, his ministry. This is how he can lead by example as Jesus did.

Deacons

The first Scripture passage in the New Testament that speaks of a need for the supporting functions of deacons is Acts 6:1-6. Some observations concerning these verses will help provide a valid understanding of this ministry.

• The primary need was not to perform a menial task but to maintain proper relationships between Hebrew and Greek believers. It involved a limited degree of shepherding.

• The choice of men was based on certain qualifications (full of the Spirit and wisdom, having a good reputation), qualities the people themselves could recognize, and by which they were to select them. Thus, they were approved by the people for ministry primarily on the basis of their characters.

● They were appointed (or set in place) by the apostles. Responsibility for relationship in the church lay with the twelve apostles, and they delegated their authority for this task to these men.

The end results of their ministry served to support the apostolic ministry of teaching and prayer.

Deacons function out of the authority of the elders who set them in place; their role is not to be viewed as permanent but is subject to change both because of the growth and needs of the assembly and their own spiritual growth. Delegated functions should *never* be viewed as "non-spiritual" in nature, because they are a necessary part of the spiritual whole that comprises shepherding. Some of the better known and more commonly accepted responsibilities of deacons are the following:

● financial (bookkeeping, insurance, records, etc.)
● building facilities and maintenance
● transportation requirements
● publishing (printing, distribution, tape duplication and libraries, etc.)
● assembly responsibilities (welcoming new people, meeting notices, housing arrangements, etc.)

Although such functions require commitment and faithfulness, they have limited value for training those who, like Philip, have a call of God to one of the five ministries listed in Ephesians 4:11.

The following are other examples of responsibilities that can be delegated to those being trained for leadership. Being more directly a part of the shepherding role, they afford opportunity for men to grow in this type of ministry. The key element in each instance is a component of personal interaction and involvement in the lives of others. These activities can be classrooms of practical learning.

● outreach ministry (coffeehouse, evangelistic endeavors, etc.)

- children's ministry
- jail and hospital ministries, as well as homes for those with needs that require family or community support, i.e., drug addiction
- home church leadership

Each candidate for leadership in these functions should be one whose life priorities have become properly adjusted. His personal life, home life and financial life are to be in order. With some exceptions, this means being free of debt (excluding the mortgage on his home). No one should be considered for full-time support until he has demonstrated a consistent pattern of successful ministry while working to provide his own support, as well as contributing to the needs of others. Where possible the oversight of home churches should be assigned to at least two leaders who are to serve and oversee one another while being responsible to those over them in the Lord. The practice develops an understanding of how to flow in plural leadership. They will learn how to receive and give correction and to encourage and build up what they see lacking in their co-workers. Over time, their commitment to those with whom they are yoked will grow into a visible reality and be an example to the ones they are serving. When personality conflicts arise, each instance becomes a battleground that must be won if the ministry is to mature. Heart attitudes will surface that must be dealt with in honest confrontations. Spiritual competition and a desire for personal recognition (often seen in attitudes that say, "Look, I am more experienced, so do as I say") are human characteristics that are out of place in a servant of Christ. Hearts must be stretched to receive one another just as Christ received us.

Delegation of oversight for such functions should not be done lightly. In particular, the selection of leaders requires much time and prayer. False starts can be expected. This is probably what Paul had in mind in his exhortation to Timothy on deacons:

> *And let these also **first be tested**; then let them serve as deacons if they are above reproach.*
>
> First Timothy 3:10

As with elders, their qualifications are more focused on character and home life than on ability to perform in ministry.

> *Deacons likewise must be men of dignity, not double-tongued, or addicted to much wine or fond of sordid gain, but holding to the mystery of the faith with a clear conscience... Women* [including deacon's wives or deaconesses] *must likewise be dignified, not malicious gossips, but temperate, faithful in all things. Let deacons be husbands of only one wife, and good managers of their children and their own households. For those who have served well as deacons obtain for themselves a high standing and great confidence in the faith that is in Christ Jesus.*
>
> First Timothy 3:8-9, 11-13

There are many principles and maxims one could set down for operating "home groups"; however, I am not sure all would apply in each assembly. In general, the small groups are "practice grounds" for body ministry, confrontation and exercising responsibility. Above all, they are places to grow up in a kind of "spiritual hot house." It has been my experience that when a new believer comes to share from the pulpit in the large central meeting, it is good to know how well he shares in his home church. If he cannot minister life there, it is unlikely he would do so in the larger meeting. Home leaders, as well as elders, must learn to firmly but gently restrain the "pushy extrovert" who always has something to say.

They must also learn to recognize the difference between a rebel and one who opposes out of honest conviction. A rebel is one who will not let anyone into his life so that he can be confronted and corrected. There is little you can do to help such a person except to wait for God to bring him into circumstances that cause him to cry out for help.

The meeting format and the assignment of people to home groups should be flexible. People ought to be allowed to change home churches for personal reasons, but never for the purpose of running from a problem. Although the attendees have great freedom to share in the meetings, they must recognize that the Church is *not* a democracy. There is a valid spiritual oversight present at all times, one for which the eldership is responsible in the eyes of the Lord. Finally, there should not be home churches specifically for singles, for young marrieds, for teenagers, etc. Although such meetings are historically common, they can hinder personal growth. Each cell group should be a true cross section of the assembly as much as possible and families should remain together.

Any house where a ministry function is located *must* be a home in spiritual order with God's peace resting upon it. Since the husband of that family is responsible for whatever occurs there, he should be one of the leaders if possible. Regular periods of mutual sharing, teaching and counseling should be set aside by the elders with these respective leaders. This is needed to ensure that there is a valid flow of life taking place, both in the people and in those serving in leadership. A meeting with all the necessary mechanics, but which produces no life over time, has little value and should be terminated. In addition, there must be a consistency maintained in any personal counseling offered within these groups with that coming from the elders. Counsel in a home group can only extend as far as its leaders have achieved victory in their own lives; whatever is beyond this level must be handled by the eldership.

Some may find it difficult to see home churches functioning under the oversight of deacons, or that of men not yet set in as elders. However, it should be recognized that these meetings are not miniature versions of the main central gatherings. When the whole church comes together, it is (from a ministry point of view) to hear what God is saying through a prophetic flow of worship, gifts and teaching. Home churches are places where that word is worked out in lives, including the training of those overseeing the groups. If we consider where churches in general have failed, it is not so much in what has been preached as in the failure to obey the Word. Home churches provide an excellent atmosphere to do just this. Rather than teaching, emphasis should be on establishing an atmosphere where there is mutual support to help each other grow in Christ. Everyone in an assembly, including those called to ascension-gift ministries, must grow and develop. A fellowship is always changing as people grow, and it is exciting to see apostolic and prophetic qualities develop in men who have proven faithful as home group leaders. Responsibility is a part of the training. Home meetings can involve worship, prayer, testimonies, evangelism, exhortation, spiritual gifts, communion, table fellowship, working together, recreation and, in general, sharing together the practical as well as spiritual areas of lives. "What I am and what I possess belong to the Lord, so let me share with you," becomes the primary focus of ministry. The meeting oversight, therefore, is not so much concerned with directive ministry as it is with ensuring that nothing hinders the flow of life coming forth as the people open their hearts to the Lord. Occasional teaching sessions by elders will be necessary to address specific needs and subjects. Prayer and worship must undergird all meetings. They are the first priority. The objectives of home churches are essentially threefold:

1. To help one another walk in personal victory with Christ.

2. To attain a victorious corporate (group or collective) redemption in relationship with one another. This will entail many nitty-gritty aspects of personal interaction, tensions, confrontations and ministries of relationship.

3. Evangelism; the group is a witness to neighbors of the love of Christ through personal testimonies and their love for

one another (John 13:34; 17:21-23). They demonstrate the gospel as a community as well as preaching it individually. Additional groups will be formed out of new converts once there is adequate leadership for them. Thus, an assembly can multiply in numbers as it divides into more and more cell groups or home churches. However, there must be continual emphasis on the quality of what is built, rather than on numbers. Evangelism is the primary reason why home meetings should not be closed in attendance. A church without a vision and strategy for evangelism will be a failure.

Those put in charge of home churches, where possible, should be those men who appear most likely to have calls from God to become evangelists, prophets, teachers, pastors, etc. This period of limited responsibility will serve to prepare them for their later ministry. It serves both to give proof of their ministry and to develop the character necessary to support it. This includes proving faithful in such things as employment, proper management of their households and good relationships with people, both in and outside the church. It is these things that require so much time, which prompted Paul's warning concerning novices (1 Tim. 3:6). In the context of training, it is more correct to speak of discipling rather than education — to speak of "watch my example," rather than "learn this concept." The discipling of Timothy by Paul is a good example of such training since it included the practical aspects of their traveling together for several years.

One ingredient our assembly has consistently experienced in home meetings is change. This is not bad and should be expected, for growth means change. There will always be new people, new problems and new challenges. Leaders are given responsibilities consistent with their walks, available time and family responsibilities, each of which can change over time. New groups may require "seed" people to get started. Finally, it is necessary to ensure that no cliques form within a group. What is a correct direction for one group may not be for others. Spiritual life demands that we *always* be ready to change.

I suspect it is a common failure not to move men into places of delegated responsibility soon enough. We tend to look for all qualifications to be visible first. However, God sees the heart; He alone knows the needs of the people, how these needs can be met, and how the responsibility and difficulties involved can help mature the candidate. There is no set of cut-and-dried rules; each decision must be birthed out of the heart of God. If those being trained can see the elders flowing together in a united, submitted covering, it is easier to receive admonishment from them in the course of training. Example is a wonderful textbook!

The role of sisters who serve as deaconesses is more important than most realize, probably because their work is usually done in the background, and is thus less visible than that of men. However, Paul made it clear in his epistle to the Romans how valuable their work was to him personally as well as to the church (Rom. 16:1-6). The ministry of women in the assembly does *not* include exercising authority over men; for this reason they are not part of the eldership (1 Tim. 2:12). The reason for this command of the Lord is that spiritual headship be maintained in the church (1 Cor. 11:3). The first sin ever committed (by Lucifer) and the first sin by man arose out of failure in this area. For this reason, women are to have authority (not a symbol or token of authority, for such a word is *not* present in the Greek) on their head when they minister; they must be spiritually covered by man, either their husband or the elders, so that they are not deceived as Eve was.

Married sisters should recognize that, although they have their individual gifts and anointings, the greatness of their ministry lies in the completeness they bring to their husbands' ministries. Together, they represent a spiritual unit in the body of Christ which is greater than their two separate ministries. This is true whether her ministry is more home-oriented or is a visible, public ministry exercised under the covering of her husband. Godly wives are the glory of their husbands (2 Cor. 11:7).

> *An excellent wife is the crown of her husband...*
>
> Proverbs 12:4

Her goal is that her life and acts "praise her in the gates," which is where her husband sits, and that his heart trusts in her.

> *Her husband is known in the gates when he sits among the elders of the land. ...Give her the product* [fruits] *of her hands, and let her works praise her in the gates.*
>
> Proverbs 31:23, 31

God has greatly blessed me with a wife who abundantly fulfils these Scriptures, and I testify to their truth.

Elders and Traveling Ministries

The relationship between elders and traveling ministries is probably best understood by recognizing the three growth phases that should occur for each assembly.

1. The first stage is the *birth* or *evangelistic phase.* Through outreach ministry (such as that of Philip at Samaria recorded in Acts 8:5-17) people are brought to repentance, converted to Christ, and baptized in water and the Holy Spirit. One might say at this point that material has been assembled to build a local expression of the body of Christ, and there are no prefabricated walls! This phase will continue through a period of teaching and instruction. Responsibility for the people lies in the one who has fathered them in Christ. Ideally, that person (or persons) will have been sent out from another assembly and will report back for prayer and other support as needed. This phase is primarily concerned with each convert's personal relationship with the Lord; in time there will be instruction on the believers' relationships together and what it means to be committed members of the body of Christ. If the

vertical relationship, as described in Chapter Two, is not in order, there will be no valid corporate growth later on.

2. The second stage can be thought of as the "*diakonate*". What has been lacking in the assembly up to this point is local leadership. When elders are eventually set in place, the assembly can begin to function as a local expression of the body of Christ. At this time, the assembly begins to express the life of Christ in caring for itself through shepherding.

> *For this reason I left you in Crete, that you might set in order what remains, and **appoint elders in every city** as I directed you.*
>
> Titus 1:5

> *And when they [Barnabas and Paul] had **appointed elders** for them **in every church**, having prayed with fasting, they commended them to the Lord in whom they had believed.*
>
> Acts 14:23

This phase doesn't occur just because "having elders" is a proper thing to do. It is the end result of teaching the people on the bond of covenant relationship they have been called into and the care they are to have for one another. In time, some men in the assembly will begin to manifest a concern for others, caring for and feeding them. These will be recogized as men called into shepherding roles. Sheep will follow those who serve them; leaders are simply those whom others follow. Setting elders in place is the public recognition of what God has already worked in their hearts. This does not imply that the assembly is now a mature church, but rather that a proper foundation has been laid upon which lives can build and mature together in Christ.

Apostolic and prophetic ministries, if not prominent in the first phase, will be in this one; everything built in the future must be supported on this foundation being laid (1 Cor. 3:10). It is only when the foundation has been completed that men who have committed themselves to what God is doing among the people and have the Lord's anointing upon them for leadership will be appointed as elders to shepherd the flock. These men must meet the qualifications for character set forth in Scripture, and should have a call to one of the five ministries of Ephesians 4:11. From this point on, the responsibility for that assembly rests on these elders who share the oversight equally. Submission to the Lord and to one another has been a key part of the foundation built in their lives. Because of this, they should be able to provide the oversight and correction needed in one another's lives so they can walk in victory and be above reproach in their lives. Collegial sharing of responsibility for oversight serves to keep Jesus preeminent in His rightful place as the "Chief Shepherd" (1 Pet. 5:4) and the "Wonderful Counsellor" (Isa. 9:6) of the assembly. Collegiality in eldership prevents the church from being under the inordinate influence of one man. It also sets an example to the flock of how they are to submit to one another (Eph. 5:21). It is easy for the sheep to follow men who go before them demonstrating a commitment to serve one another and who stand united in shepherding them. They are visible as men who are both *in* authority and *under* authority. To be under the authority of someone in a distant assembly, one who is not a part of your everyday life, can only be of very limited value. As the need arises, elders will be responsible for bringing into the assembly various traveling ministries to help equip the saints for service. A "child-father" relationship should continue to exist between the elders and the one who fathered their assembly so that instruction and correction can be offered from time to time (such as the relationship that existed between Paul and the church at Corinth).

Two common practices should be avoided when building an eldership:

a. Do not make a man an elder on the basis of administrative abilities alone. He should have the grace of one of the five ascension gift ministries.

b. Do not set one elder at a level of authority over the other elders (i.e. as pastor or "senior pastor"). There is a temptation to do this since it is a quick way to put a local church government into place. It is better to take extra time and build the character necessary for a collegial eldership.

Both practices can frustrate and hinder the raising up of new ascension gift ministries from the men being trained.

3. The third stage of growth can be considered the *"fatherhood phase."* Although the local elders share responsibility equally in the assembly, it soon becomes evident that their ministries are different. The diversity and distinction in ministry graces should grow over time. Also, certain of the men will be released from secular employment so they can give themselves fully to their ministries. Eventually, it will become apparent that one or more have become concerned with building the body of Christ on a trans-local basis; their vision has expanded from the immediate locality to areas beyond.

Their ministry has not *changed,* but it has been *extended in dimension.* It is now apostolic. The Lord begins to open doors for them to minister in new places. This may involve a "planting" ministry through evangelism, or a "watering" ministry that builds up and equips saints in other assemblies. These two ministry orientations, that of an "inward vision" and an "outward vision," are both valid and necessary. The presence of both emphases in leadership serves to ensure a proper balance between missionary outreach and local assembly development as parts of the total vision imparted to the church. This phase is a necessary one if a church is to multiply. Ministries are birthed from the womb of local assemblies, and new assemblies are in turn birthed by these ministries. This is the life cycle by which Christ builds His Church. For this reason, apostolic and prophetic ministries *can be expected to emerge* from the eldership of an assembly. Such men should be encouraged in their ministries and released by their peers; having been sent out, they are to report back on the fruits of their ministry (Acts 14:26-28). Recognition of their ministry should be made solely on the basis of the fruits it produces. It will be only as valid as what is built in the lives of those to whom they minister. If they have been birthed from a "New Testament" assembly, they should be able to lay a foundation for such an assembly to be built in the lives of others.

It will not be easy for elders to trust one another and flow together in harmony when they see this separation in vision. However, it is primarily these very differences the Lord uses to melt hearts together in a stronger covering of the flock. It is this diversity in stature and ministry that more completely reflects Christ to the church. An eldership made up of men who were alike in their ministry callings (e.g., all teachers) would be less effective in equipping the saints. A mature eldership will recognize that there are men among them who are given to the *whole* Church, not just one assembly. Each leader must learn he cannot be independent; the Lord's ministers are not "Lone Rangers." We need one another much more than we realize. What a contrast such a relationship provides when compared to each one doing his own thing, seeking personal recognition, and putting down others who function differently!

As long as those with the "outward vision" are resident and ministering locally, they are seen as elders. Each contributes the life of Christ within him as a unique enrichment of local shepherding (i.e., prophecy, teaching, counseling, etc.). When they travel, they are to be received for their specific ministries, which the anointing upon them uniquely contributes toward equipping the saints. For example, Peter was recognized as both an apostle and an elder (1 Pet. 5:1); Judas and Silas were elders at Jerusalem, but when they traveled they were prophets (Acts 15:22-32). Timothy is often described as a "young pastor," however, Paul identified his ministry as apostolic (1 Thess. 1:1; 2:6). His epistles to Timothy included instruction on evangelism and subjects related to the divine order of assemblies, those concerns that an experienced father would impart to a young "masterbuilder." Acts chapters 13 and 14 provide an excellent record of the outward vision and ministry of Paul and Barnabas from the church at Antioch.

The dangers of self-deception are very real! Each of us needs to be *continually* open to input from others concerning our walk and ministry; there is no place for "wandering apostles" who go from place to place doing their thing and being subject to no one. Those who are sent out are responsible to those who released them for the scope and purpose of their ministry. When they return to their home base, they are once again united with their peers in the eldership. Their personal life is thus *always* open to inspection. Traveling ministries, as much as possible, should be in pairs for reasons of protection, encouragement, training and breadth of ministry. We can expect to see many teams of apostolic and prophetic ministries raised up in the years ahead.

Traveling ministries are men who have been *sent* by the Holy Spirit and who have been *released* by a local church (Acts 13:1-4). They are not to become permanent in extralocal ministry; it is necessary that they periodically return, not only for reasons of accountability, but also for their contributions to the strategy of the home church.

In general there are two options for sending out apostolic ministry from an established local church:

a. An apostle could be released, along with a prophet and other supporting ministries, as an apostolic team to plant new expressions in distant places. They would remain with each new body until it was established.

b. An apostolic minister could travel out on frequent trips to locations close to home to plant new churches. In this labor, he would take along other ministries and men in training to assist him. They would not be resident on a permanent basis in these new sites but would return from time to time until men could be trained and set in place as elders.

Both methods are valid, but the first one has two concerns that should be addressed before being pursued. The one being sent should not leave *before* an apostolic or fathering ministry is evident in the home assembly and he must be sure he does *not* travel beyond the God-appointed sphere of his responsibility.

Commitment to Serve

The early Church preached a greater call to commitment than we are accustomed to today. Evangelists are not to bring people to Christ and then go off and leave them. Those we lead to Jesus we are to serve until Christ becomes Lord of their lives (or relate them to a group where this can happen). In turn, they are expected to respond by committing themselves to the local church. Paul's epistle to the Corinthians points out this truth:

> *For we do not preach ourselves but Christ Jesus as Lord, and ourselves as your bond-servants for Jesus' sake.*
>
> Second Corinthians 4:5

> *...this, not as we had expected, but they first gave themselves to the Lord and to us by the will of God.*
>
> Sesond Corinthians 8:5

In essence, Paul said: "We have led you to Christ; He is to become Lord in your life. We are proclaiming ourselves to be your servants, so that we can help this come to pass."

This depth of commitment should mark *every* elder's heart; it is a commitment that can be read by others.

> *You are our letter, written in our hearts, known and read by all men; being manifested that you are a letter of Christ, served* [cared for] *by us...*
>
> Second Corinthians 3:2-3

If you are a shepherd, people will be able to "look into your heart" and see the lives of those you serve and care for.

They will hear it in your words, for it will be your passion. I can testify that this is true in the lives of the fellow elders with whom I am yoked. A commitment to serve in the *diakonate* means you are willing for your heart to be seen as a "carbon copy" of the letter being written in the lives of those you are serving. This is the kind of relationship that should also exist between the elders and those responsible men of the assembly being trained in ministry.

A good example of this can be found in the ministry of Elisha. The greatest miracle accomplished by Elijah was the building of his ministry into Elisha. One can read the record of Elisha's miracles and see in them the pattern of Elijah's earlier ministry, but on a greater scale and without Elijah's failure (i.e., running from Jezebel and believing himself to be the only righteous one in Israel). In a similar way, each succeeding generation of ministry should be one of ascension (not the declension seen in church history). There will be greater results from the young men God is calling into ministry today than from their fathers. Elisha spent much time with Elijah, learning from him and serving him. His commitment to receiving the anointing of Elijah, so vividly expressed in the record of Second Kings chapter two, is a testimony to all who are called into His service.

Paul's discipling of the men who became elders at Ephesus provides great insight into the dimensions and depth of such training.

> *Therefore be on the alert, remembering that night and day for a period of three years I did not cease to admonish each one with tears.*

Acts 20:31

For three years Paul daily poured out his heart to establish these men in the areas of their personal character and relationship together, so they would be able to stand as one man in shepherding the Church. His teaching was not confined to character and ministry, for he also unveiled the eternal purposes of God for the Church.

> *For I did not shrink from declaring to you the whole purpose of God.*

Acts 20:27

Furthermore, he lived before them the gospel he preached. His life was an example of how they were to serve one another and the flock.

> *You yourselves know that these hands ministered to my own needs and to the men who were with me.* ***In everything I showed you that by working hard in this manner you must help the weak*** *and remember the words of the Lord Jesus, that He Himself said, "It is more blessed to give than to receive."*

Acts 20:34-35

I personally can testify to the great blessing it was over the years to minister the gospel freely and not use the privilege of financial support. It is a mistake to think that once we are called into ministry we are never to do secular work. Like Paul at Ephesus, there will be occasions when this is how we can best demonstrate our commitment to those we serve. By so doing, we, like Paul, can set an example for those God would raise up into leadership (2 Thess. 3:8-9). If we have given up everything to fulfill our call, then we must also be willing to give up the privilege of financial support at times. Otherwise, there will be many small places where ministry will never come.

Paul did not minister alone but was accompanied by others assisting him and also being trained. Ministry teams were very common in the early Church; some examples are given in the following Scriptures: Acts 8:14, Acts 13:2, Acts 15:27, Acts 16:1-4, Acts 18:5, Acts 19:22, 2 Cor. 1:19, 1 Cor. 16:17, and Col. 4:7-9. These all speak of a spirit of cooperation that was present.

The Priority of Ministry

Whether single or married with a family, each believer is responsible for the stewardship of his time. The important thing is to recognize the correct priorities for using it. The proper order is: the Lord first, our family second, and then ministry or work as led by the Lord.

There are two snares one must seek to avoid concerning the priority of ministry:

1. To assume that because one is called into ministry, he should no longer do secular work. It is *not always* ministry before work.

2. To put ministry ahead of our family responsibilities. I was guilty of this for many years, and it became a source of great mental and physical stress to my wife. Because she was so capable in homemaking and caring for the children, I let many responsibilities fall on her shoulders that I should have borne. This was especially true in training and disciplining the children. The Lord had to adjust my life in this area. This took time since it was a problem I did not see clearly at first. Habit patterns and life styles are not changed overnight.

Chapter Six

Training the Diakonate

Faithful Men

You therefore, my son, be strong in the grace that is in Christ Jesus. And the things which you have heard from me in the presence of many witnesses, these entrust to faithful men, who will be able to teach others also.

Second Timothy 2:1

These words of Paul were written to instruct Timothy as to how to train and raise up men into leadership. We notice first that he did not outline some curriculum of formal studies in which those who proved themselves more academically gifted would be selected. Men are to be chosen on the basis of three things. First, they must be faithful. They need not necessarily be highly intelligent or well-educated, but they must have proven faithful with what has been entrusted to them. Secondly, they must have God's anointing which enables them to impart what they have received to others. Finally, they should be secure in their call.

This is the heart of discipleship: to pass on to others the fruit and substance of the life of Christ we have come to experience from our personal relationship with Him. If all we have to offer is theoretical concepts and interpretations of His ways, that is all we will impart to others, and it will not go far in building the Church. Paul pointed Timothy to those things that he had heard Paul teach over the years. The phrase "in the presence of many witnesses" suggests that this most likely involved those periods of instruction where Paul laid foundations for new churches. We know that Timothy traveled with him for the purpose of being trained through both ministry and personal example. Corinth, Philippi, Colossae and Thessalonica were cities where Timothy came in the company of Paul and undoubtedly heard teaching and witnessed the training of potential elders similar to what we know was given to the leaders at Ephesus. It was practical demonstrations of the character and ministry of this man, so strong in the grace of God, that constituted Timothy's Bible school. Much of the life of Christ within Paul was built into Timothy during the times they traveled together. In essence, Paul's counsel for Timothy was to repeat this process and build into other men what the Lord had established in him. He was encouraged not to rely on his own skill and natural talents but to find strength in the grace of God.

I am sure we all would be delighted to have details of the content and structure of Paul's teaching on the training of men. It would be easier to follow a well-defined scriptural program. It is a mark of our humanity to seek the easiest way to achieve goals. However, it is apparent that if we did adopt such a set of procedures, it would eventually become a standard for examinations by which candidates would be tested. Life is not imparted by education alone, for knowledge by itself produces arrogance. The proof of successful training is when the godly character of a bond-servant has been developed.

The Ladder of Serving

Doubtless there are many scriptural approaches one could set forth as acceptable methods to view the spiritual growth and ministry of those whom the Lord brings into leadership. The following is a simple scriptural format or word picture that outlines the dimensions of such training in a way that is easily understood. It assumes that a plural, collegial leadership structure exists or is the objective, so that there are no "bottle-necks" or hindrances to raising up new ministries.

Figure 1 pictures a ladder with seven rungs, where each rung denotes a level of serving in the house of the Lord. Some workers will stand only on the first rung, others will stand on the first two rungs and so on, until at the top of the ladder all seven rungs represent the range of service expected from elders.

There will be little fruit in his service if a minister's heart is tainted by pride and he is unable to receive correction, or lacks the commitment to serve others. For this reason, the longitudinal arms of the ladder have been labeled "character" and "commitment." These are two personal qualities that must be focused on in the discipling of new converts, for they are traits that in the end will qualify or validate their ministries in the eyes of those for whom it is intended. For this reason, they are shown as the two sides of the ladder that provide support for each rung. The rungs denote the various inter-personal aspects of ministry that take place in a normal assembly, particularly in home churches.

Each rung is described by the Greek word for a specific action or ministry that expresses a degree of involvement or personal interaction between parties. A rung therefore implies some level of service where spiritual life is imparted to others; the seven rungs represent an increasing degree or depth in serving as one proceeds from the lowest rung to the top of the ladder. The ladder thus represents a framework for discipling men by which the growth of those being trained can be observed, and it also provides a practical way to identify those who may be called into a *diakonate.*

Before we examine each rung, I would point out that other words could have been selected, for they are simply representative of a level of personal interaction. Furthermore, I recognize that the translation of these words into English varies between different versions of the Bible.

Rungs of Service

Let us examine each rung in the light of relational dynamics when it occurs in the normal flow of body life.

1. *Elegcho*: "to convict or to reprove."

The base from which ministry is to spring forth in new Christians is their walk in newness of life. As they walk in the light of the Lord, their conduct becomes a reproof to their acquaintances and associates outside the Church who still walk in darkness. This level does not involve any significant ministry of the Word. It is not even necessary that they speak in reproof, because their life of righteousness is a reproof to the ungodly.

Within the Church, their new life can be expressed through simple testimonies, the spirit of prophecy and sharing of Christ. This dimension of ministry is the heart of Paul's exhortation to the Christians at Ephesus (Eph. 5:1-15). Ministry within this context can be used by the Lord in meetings to convict those present who are unbelievers or untaught in God's righteousness (1 Cor. 14:24). This dimension of ministry requires no training in homiletics since it is largely impersonal in nature. It flows from a life filled with the Spirit, one whose walk is being conformed to the way of righteousness. Establishing this level of life-flow should precede *all* other training for ministry. It is a great mistake to put new Christians to work so that by being busy they will be kept interested, especially when their personal lives are still out of order. New believers know the *price* of their salvation, but they must also understand the *value* of it. It is to be of great value to *Him*. Anything that I have received as a result of my salvation, which I esteem as valuable, has no real value *unless* it glorifies Christ. I have heard Christians boast of becoming wealthy because they had faith to believe promises of prosperity. Unless such wealth brings glory to the Lord, it is valueless in the kingdom. Much of what is done in christendom brings little value to Him. This can happen when there is too strong an emphasis on one part of the gospel such as deliverance or healing. The first concern, therefore, must be to establish the values of a redeemed life in such basic things as family order, commitment, habit patterns and general conduct before being concerned with developing any directive ministry to others.

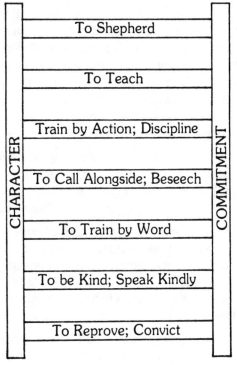

Figure 1
The Ladder of Serving

- To Shepherd
- To Teach
- Train by Action; Discipline
- To Call Alongside; Beseech
- To Train by Word
- To be Kind; Speak Kindly
- To Reprove; Convict

CHARACTER — COMMITMENT

— INCREASING PERSONAL INTERACTION →

2. The second rung is identified by two words: *eleeo,* meaning "to be kind" or "to have mercy," and *paramutheomai,* which means "to speak kindly."

This rung represents ministry at the first level of personal interaction for new Christians. It relates as much to *how* to speak as to *what* to say. The zeal of some new saints can provoke disasters as they seek to impart truth. However, good judgment comes from experience, and experience comes from bad judgments. In time they learn that others feed on our spirit as well as our words and that both must be in harmony when we speak for the Lord. This ministry level should be seen as one that is simple and uncomplicated. Some applications include teaching children and bringing instruction to the elderly or infirm. I have a mentally retarded son, and many times he has been richly ministered to by those who spoke kindly to him, even though he often did not receive the sense of what they said. Everyone can talk about Christ, but not everyone can speak for Him.

> *And we urge you,, brethren...**encourage** [lit: speak kindly to] **the fainthearted** [lit: feebleminded, or of little soul], **help the weak...***
>
> First Thessalonians 5:14

Those responsible to train and equip saints for ministry are to see this rung as an integral part of the "bridle phase" that new disciples go through, where personal characteristics that would hinder a flow of life in their words are effectively dealt with. It also represents a level of growth where new Christians are better equipped for their witness to the lost.

> *But sanctify Christ as Lord in your hearts, always being ready to make a defense to everyone who asks you to give an account for the hope that is in you, yet with **gentleness and reverence.***
>
> First Peter 3:15

3. ***Noutheteo***, "to put in mind," "to train by word," "to warn."

Noutheteo is often the verb in Scriptures that are rich in the life flow of worship and body ministry.

> *Let the word of Christ richly dwell within you, with all*
> *wisdom teaching and **admonishing** one another with*
> *psalms and hymns and spiritual songs...*
>
> Colossians 3:16

This rung of the ladder provides a testing for growing Christians to see whether or not they minister life when they bring input into the lives of others. This will happen once there has been sufficient spiritual growth in character to qualify their words. Much of the preparation to minister at this level will take place in home churches.

> *...I myself also am convinced that you yourselves are*
> ***full of goodness, filled with all knowledge**, and able also*
> *to **admonish** one another.*
>
> Romans 15:14

It is good for believers to "practice" such ministry in the home church until they possess the goodness and knowledge necessary to train (admonish) others in the central meetings (1 Thess. 5:14, 2 Thess. 3:14-15).

4. ***Parakaleo***, to call near (or alongside), encourage, comfort, beseech. This word implies a degree of personal interaction that is greater than simply speaking words of correct instruction to others.

Scripture verses that employ *parakaleo* in describing body ministry are ones that convey a rich flow of the Lord's life among His people (1 Thess. 4:18, 1 Cor. 14:3, 2 Cor. 7:6-7, 13; Col. 22:2).

It is one thing to inform someone that their house is on fire; it is another thing to tell them it is on fire and that you are there to help put it out. Similarly, we can speak a redemptive word, and because we have been through the problem ourselves we minister it in such a way that we "come alongside" to assist. In short, the word suggests a greater ability and personal willingness to help those to whom it is spoken.

Not forsaking our own assembling together, as is the habit of some, but encouraging one another; and all the more, as you see the day drawing near.

Hebrews 10:25

Therefore encourage one another, and build up one another, just as you also are doing.

First Thessalonians 5:11

Finally, brethren, rejoice, be made complete, be comforted, be like-minded, live in peace; and the God of love and peace shall be with you.

Second Corinthians 13:11

These verses imply a genuine capability to help one another. It is in overcoming personal problems that we learn to appropriate the Lord's strength that in turn enables us to help others. This is vividly portrayed in Paul's words to the Corinthian church:

Blessed be the God...of all comfort; who comforts us in all our affliction so that we may be able to comfort those who are in any affliction with the comfort we ourselves are comforted by God.

Second Corinthians 1:3-4

But encourage one another day after day, as long as it is still called "Today," lest any one of you be hardened by the deceitfulness of sin.

Hebrews 3:13

From men who manifest a consistent witness of the life of Christ at this rung, some can be selected and delegated authority to oversee the endeavors of small groups of believers (such as home meetings.). These men represent a first level of the *diakonate* in the eyes of the congregation. It will be from such men that the eldership will recognize those who have the call of God to come eventually into an ascension-gift ministry.

5. *Paideuo,* "to train by action," "to discipline," "to chasten."

There is no Scripture to support members of the body of Christ disciplining one another. However, the word does apply in the training of our children (Heb. 12:9-10; Eph. 6:4). When Christian parents have the fruits of the first four rungs evident in their lives, the exercise of discipline is much more likely to be seen as an expression of love by their children.

After a baby is born, and while he is in the diaper phase, parents don't think of discipline, but rather of love and care. Once the child is able to understand their wishes, they begin to exercise discipline. So it is in our relationship with the Lord. We are loved and cared for as newborn children; initially, our training is largely by instruction. However, there comes a time when we recognize our adoption as sons; this is when we face His discipline, which is to conform us into His image. We must then choose either to remain rebels or to embrace the privileges of sonship. As sons we are never too old to escape the benefit of discipline. Once we have embraced the Lord's discipline, we are able to help others do so.

The Lord cannot use leaders as instruments to minister discipline until they themselves have grown and matured through all that is represented by the first four rungs. The Lord's action in our discipline is always out of a heart of love; likewise, home group leaders must be men after His heart who, from experience, truly understand His redemptive acts among the group. Their action in any discipline must be remedial for both the group and the involved person(s), and it must be supported by the eldership. *Paideuo* can occasionally be an active element in counseling.

6. *Didasko*: "to teach."

Didasko is not used in the Scriptures to describe members of the body of Christ giving directive instruction to one another. However, it is used to define the teaching content in a prophetic flow of worship and body ministry. It will also be present in those who are overseeing home churches.

*Let the word of Christ richly dwell within you, with all wisdom **teaching** and admonishing one another with psalms hymns and spiritual songs, singing with thankfulness in your hearts to God.*

Colossians 3:16

A normal assembly in its growth process should eventually bring forth teachers as well as the other ministries. This was a concern expressed in the epistle to the Hebrews; as an assembly they had not matured as expected. They were not able to teach one another foundation truths and still needed teachers to again provide such input (Heb. 5:12-14). Elders are to recognize those in the home churches upon whom an anointing rests for such ministry and develop this aspect of His life flow in them. As young men embrace the call of God to the ministry, an ascension-gift grace will become evident in their lives *before* they attain the maturity and experience necessary for eldership. Such anointing should be recognized, and their ministry developed in concert with their personal character *prior to* assuming the responsibility of eldership. However, there will be some who excel at teaching who may never have a shepherd's heart. Under proper oversight, these men can assist the elders in feeding the flock and overseeing home churches.

7. *Pomaino*, "to tend as a shepherd."

The word *pomaino* is not used in reference to any ministry between non-leaders in the body of Christ. However, there are Scriptures that speak of a deep caring for one another. Such caring grows out of learning to serve at the first five rungs. Some examples are Galations 6:1-2 and Hebrews 12:12-15. When the life expressed in these or similar verses is consistently seen in someone and there is an anointing for ministry at rung six, then we are looking at one who is a potential elder. He has covered the practical and spiritual syllabus for those being trained in the Lord's seminary.

This seventh rung embraces the whole range of services required of elders to bear the burden of the Lord's house.

No one can be a good shepherd without also being a sheep; to be *in authority* we must also be under authority. Unless I am willing to be shepherded, I cannot expect the Lord to anoint me to oversee the lives of others. One reason Jesus is the Good Shepherd is that He was first the "good Lamb." He came to earth as the Lamb of God and was obedient to the shepherding of His Father. As a consequence He has been exalted as King of kings and Lord of lords. It is the lamblike nature of Jesus that marks His greatness as our Shepherd. This quality should be true for elders as well.

*For the **Lamb** in the center of the throne shall be their **Shepherd**, and shall guide them to springs of the water of life...*

Revelation 7:17

I remember the first time my son corrected me in the Lord. It has been a great joy for me to see him called into the ministry and finally into eldership. Suddenly I found that, although we were still father and son, we were also now each other's shepherd. As a result I have experienced the Lord's correction through him on several occasions. Because he saw some of my shortcomings as a father, he has a unique insight into my family life and his input has been a great blessing to me. Spiritual stature, experience and visibility in ministry will always be reasons for the diversity that should exist in the eldership; however, the human heart is too easily deceived for anyone to be without shepherding.

No one in the *diakonate* is without oversight; this is the heart and strength of the collegial nature of eldership. I will never forget the time when the elders who were my shepherds asked me to lay down all ministry during the summer for the benefit of my family. My wife and I had a delightful time in those eight weeks, working together on the house and going out for lunch and dinner together; it was second honeymoon. It served to produce much fruit in my marital and family relationships.

In general, it is good counsel for men who are planning to marry, and who have leadership responsibility in the church, to lay down their ministry for a period of time and give themselves to establishing their marriages.

Summary

In review, each believer is called to a place of service in the Church. Elders and deacons serve the body by ministry and example to bring each member fully into the relationships with Christ and one another to which they have been called. This is best accomplished within the context of home churches that are under proper oversight. Out of this service new ministries come forth. Traveling ministries are sent out to plant new expressions of the Church, appoint elders and equip saints for their work of service. It is from such an environment that the Lord's *diakonate* will be continually raised up and His Church built.

Section Four

Building His House

THEME: The vision the Lord is that every locality be able to see His person and purposes reflected in local expressions of His body. It is not great campaigns, programs, signs and wonders or the charisma of leaders that can bring this to pass. It comes when the life and acts of God are seen in His people.

Each biological species possesses a life unique to its kind; likewise, the Church is a spiritual organism possessing the unique qualities of His life for spiritual growth and reproduction. This life order is present where His will and headship completely governs church activities. When this is the case, the diversity and spontaneity of the Holy Spirit flowing from spiritual ministries and between members is an expression of His gospel to the world. The reality and vitality of such spiritual life within a local body is sufficient to withstand adversity and persecution and to win men to Christ.

When God expresses the desire of His heart for us, and does so as our Father, it is in terms of our being His sons. When He speaks as the Son, He expresses His hearts desire for us in terms being His body or His bride. However, when He speaks as the Holy Spirit, He expresses His heart's desire in terms of our being His house, His dwelling place, His city (or place) of His rest. It is significant that this third type of expression occurs far more frequently in Scripture than either of the other two. Although they are essentially three different expressions of the same objective, the emphasis of His house points to the apostolic nature of the Lord. He is a Builder first of all. He is the Teacher, the Shepherd, the Prophet and Evangelist of our faith, but first of all He is the Apostle. This is why apostolic ministry is so necessary in the building of local churches (1 Cor. 12:28). They must be built according to the pattern of His house (Eph. 2:20-21). This pattern is set forth in the Old Testament tabernacle.

Chapter Seven

The Order of His Life

A New Wineskin

If by this point the reader is convinced that I know how to build the Lord's house, he is mistaken. Jesus is the one and only Builder; He is the Architect and the Foundation of His Church. Our part is to labor *with* Him by His grace, follow the principles of the Spirit which He reveals to us and seek His face at every point.

There is no recipe for an ideal local assembly (such as one elder for every thirty members, four deacons per elder and home churches with ten to twenty attendees). Every situation will be different, considering such things as the purposes of God for each particular expression of His body, the hearts, problems and background of the sheep, the moral environment of the community, and the vision of those who are building. However, the objective is certain; there must be a wineskin built that is adequate to contain the new wine of His life. The Lord is restoring His Church. If this wine is placed in the old wineskins that man has built over the years, they will split and the wine will be lost. The Lord will not allow this, for the loss would be too great. Neither will He patch the old wineskins (Matt. 9:15-17). He is not renovating institutions; He is building His house with stones fashioned by His life. The structure that can contain the new wine is made from disciplined lives, from living stones who are built together into a spiritual house. Any structure He builds reflects the order of His life. It is vital for those who build in His house, especially those who lay foundations, to follow the principles that bring forth and preserve this order.

I first came to understand the significance of order through revelation of the following verses:

> *For since the creation of the world His invisible attributes, His eternal power and divine nature, have been clearly seen, being understood through what has been made, so that they are without excuse.*

Romans 1:20

I understood the power of God as demonstrated through His ability to bring forth such an immense and wonderfully unique creation. I realized this did not arise out of a chance series of improbable events; it occurred through the directive words of the Lord Jesus Christ when He spoke all things into existence. I could also see His divine nature in creation. There had to be a super intelligence, far above anything human, to have put into play the complex physical laws by which the universe functions and to have brought forth life in so many expressions. However, I did not fully understand what "invisible attributes" of the Lord were to be clearly seen in the world around me until it dawned upon me that one such attribute is "order." The Godhead is a picture of divine order, where headship exists in an expression of perfect unity.

Order in Creation

As scientists probe the inner parts of matter, they continue to discover ordered arrays of particles which are the building blocks of matter and energy. When they focus telescopes toward the heavens, they again see order in the movement, dimensions and location of planets. Although we can barely grasp the magnitude of dimensions in these two worlds, the subatomic and stellar, yet both speak to us of order and a common Creator. This has encouraged me to see that result is *always* to bring forth order.

And the earth was formless and void, and darkness was over the surface of the deep...

Genesis 1:2

This is a picture of disorder. The remainder of Genesis chapter one pictures the emerging order of His handiwork. All that He created continues until this day to testify of Him.

The heavens are telling of the glory of God: and their expanse is declaring the work of His hands. Day to day pours forth speech, and night to night reveals knowledge.... Their line [sound] has gone out through all the earth, and their utterances to the end of the world...

Psalm 19:1-2, 4

This is not only true for the inanimate world; it also applies to the many types of plant and animal life. Every species, unique in appearance, function and ecology, continues to reproduce after the order of its kind. Each one is a very real part of the living whole. Creation is not disordered, but ordered, balanced and beautiful as conceived by God.

But now ask the beasts, and let them teach you; and the birds of the heavens, and let them tell you. Or speak to the earth, and let it teach you; and let the fish of the sea declare to you. Who among all these does not know that the hand of the Lord has done this, in whose hand is the life of every living thing, and the breath of all mankind?

Job 12:7-10

If all creation is a picture of order, how much more should man be, since he was created in the image of God and made to have fellowship with Him? Through sin this order has been lost. Redemption brings us back into the order of a covenant relationship with Him. The Church is spoken of in the Scriptures by several descriptive terms that denote order, such as an army, a building, a city, a bride prepared for her husband, etc. God's plan is to rule His creation by a government of order implemented under His Son and exercised through the Church.

> ...*What is man, that Thou rememberest Him? ...Thou hast crowned him with glory and honour, and hast appointed him over the works of Thy hands; Thou hast put all things in subjection under his feet.*
>
> Hebrew 2:6-8

This is the order of the future; we will only enter into it through the order of His Church that is being built today.

Disorder

To understand properly what the order of God should mean in our Christian lives we must first answer the question: "What is disorder?"

James says:

> *For where jealousy and selfish ambition exist, there is disorder...*
>
> James 3:16

Whenever we exalt ourselves to a place that was not intended by the Lord, that is disorder. When we seek to fill a place intended for someone else, that is also disorder. Spiritual competition is *always* a sign of disorder. God the Father does not compete with His Son, nor the Son with the Holy Spirit.

The word "order" embraces the concepts of both arrangement (position) and authority. The word "submission" means literally to "set in array under." When we are in total submission to His will for us, then we are in order. Disorder is anything contrary to the arrangement and authority intended by God, whether it is in the physical, human or spiritual realm.

The human concept of order is one of a stifling, hierarchal structure of government, where people live by rules and are expected to act in prescribed ways. The order of God is altogether different, for it flows out of His life. Wherever there is spiritual order, there will always exist the authority of Christ and there will always be seen the ordered harmony and diversity of His life. Just as He expressed himself creatively through the many different species of flowers, birds, butterflies, etc., He calls each member of His body to be a beautiful, unique, functional expression of His life. The Church is to radiate His glory, with each member like a jewel giving forth a distinctive color or hue, yet shining as one part of the total light. It is His life that enables us to be different, while at the same time always reflecting Him. Now, if we attempt to build our lives together, recognizing this variety but without His authority, we will produce disorder. On the other hand, if we submit to His authority but fail to recognize the various ways He would manifest His life, we will build a crippled, stereotyped, legalistic church. The order of His life has both His authority and the diversity of His Spirit expressed in diverse gifts and ministries by members of His body.

When God brought forth the first created beings, they were "set in array under" Him. There were Seraphim, Cherubim and Archangels (such as Michael and Gabriel). All of these were placed under the covering of the anointed cherub "Lucifer." This was a picture of order. The first sin, and the father of all subsequent sin, was rebellion. When Lucifer exalted himself in opposition to the will of God, he introduced disorder into the universe. We see the same picture again in the history of mankind. God created Adam and commissioned him within a framework of order. This is seen in the following observations from Genesis chapters one through three:

1. Adam was made in the likeness of God by the spirit-life breathed into him. His conduct and character were to reveal the ways of God to creation so that all would live in harmony and order with their Creator.

2. He was commissioned to rule the earth, exercising the authority given to him.

3. Since Adam was unable to fulfill this role alone, God put him to sleep, took a rib out of his body and made woman as a suitable helper for him. She completed Adam. The Lord did not breathe life into Eve, for she received her life (the life of God) from Adam. He did not commission her separately, for she received her authority with Adam, being in him when he was charged by God. Their creation and God-ordained relationship pictures for us the order of Christian marriage. Each wife has a vital and supplementary role to play in the ministry of her husband; he will not be complete without her. Her call and fulfillment are intertwined with his.

Sin and disorder came into the earth through two acts: first, Eve listened to satan and was deceived into acting without seeking her husband's counsel; and secondly, they both acted in direct disobedience to the command not to eat of the tree of knowledge of good and evil. They sought to be like God apart from His authority over them. As a result, both lost their spiritual lives. To Eve, God said, *"...and he* [Adam] *shall rule over you";* this was not an act of punishment, but a step of redemptive order.

Through sin, disorder is now manifest throughout the earth. Pollution, famines, wars, homosexuality, racism, crime, anarchy, and so on, are some of the fruits of disorder; all are contrary to the harmony and order intended by God. When we see the technocratic ingenuity of man trying to establish order apart from submission to Christ, we will always see disorder in the end. For example, we see the mechanical geometry and majesty of skyscrapers that show great engineering skill and order. However, they are surrounded by social disorders of crime and poverty. The great technological progress of industry has sapped the earth's resources, causing pollution and unbalance in our ecology. Instead of men living as brothers, we have developed divisive nationalities competing with one another, where wars are the norm for settling major disputes. Because there is no theocratic rule by God, men unite into different political parties for the purpose of government which then compete and fight with one another for the right to rule. Whenever man brings forth order in the various spheres of his carnal activities, it is always directly or indirectly followed by disorder. Only the Lord can bring forth true order. Whenever man begins to control what God is doing, the inevitable result is spiritual disorder.

We see this very clearly in the history of the Church. Beginning in the first century there began a significant falling away from the order and pattern of the New Testament Church with the apex of the fall occurring in the Dark Ages. Since that time there have been restorations of basic truths through men like Luther, Wesley and Simpson.

Although this restoration has not yet been completed, Christians since the Reformation have attempted, within the confines of their understanding, to organize order into the Church. What has resulted is the disorder of many sects and competing denominations. This is in contrast to the visible expression of Christians functioning as one body in Christ, which is the declared order of God. Correct structure, or order, can only come out of His life.

Order in Redemption

It is within the context of sin and disorder that Christ came to redeem us. Redemption will always bring order. Following the "charismatic renewal" there has been restoration of truth concerning apostles and prophets as well as local church elderships. Saints are being built together into the ordered relationship of covenant commitment. He is redeeming the Church from religious disorder and building us together in Himself as "one new man." His body is a "man of order." In contrast to Lucifer and the first Adam, who both introduced disorder, this "new man" will walk in the life and government of God. Much Christian zeal has been exerted to restore the order and pattern of the Lord's house over past years.

Although there has been a continual unfolding and restoration of lost truth, the many denominations are evidence of the disorder man has wrought by building with partial truth. It is not organization, but life, that is necessary. At present, much of the restoration is completed, and the Lord is beginning to build *visible, ordered expressions of His body* all over the earth. The whole creation, which was led into disorder by Adam, is eagerly awaiting this total restoration of man in Christ.

> *For the anxious longing of the creation waits eagerly for the revealing of the sons of God.*
>
> Romans 8:19

The sum and substance of redemption is a voluntary return, through faith in the atonement of Christ, to a place of submission and life in Him. The government of Christ will eventually fill the whole universe, bringing peace and order. The Church is the first fruits of that order.

> *And when all things are subjected to Him, then the Son Himself also will be subjected to the One who subjected all things to Him, that God may be all in all.*
>
> First Corinthians 15:28

That will be a day of perfect order!

The Order of His Government

Elders must give themselves wholeheartedly to leading the Church (by example) into the order of Christ's headship. This starts for each one in his personal relationship to Him. If this is not in order, nothing else will be. He is not interested primarily in our ministry, but in whether or not we are obedient to Him. Out of union to Him through submission His life will develop in our spirit and, in time, establish us in ministry. Furthermore, He does not bring order to our spirits and leave our souls in disorder. Our *total* life is to come into the order of God. This includes our recreational, family and secular life. It is not order on Sunday and disorder the rest of the week. Elders and deacons in a *diakonate* must be accountable to one another and be willing to have their lives overseen in a total sense throughout the week.

Once we are totally committed to Him, we will recognize that He is Lord of what comes into our lives and that our steps are being ordered by Him. We will see His hand in the circumstances or situations we encounter. My spouse, my neighbor, my boss on the job, those over me in the Lord, my brothers in Christ are seen as His instruments to set me "in array under Him." Maturity is not measured by vast knowledge of the Bible, but by how well we obey the truth we have. Understanding of new things will come as we obey what we know is expected of us. I must become visible as one walking in truth, not just as one speaking correct doctrine. We are *to be witnesses*, not simply *to witness*. This quality of life reflects the order of God. It means a good horizontal relationship with those around us, one that begins in our family environment. Whether one is at home and subject to parents or married with family responsibility, his relationship in the home must embrace the order of God. The spirit of submission we manifest in the family, as well as in our place of employment and to governmental authorities, reflects our submission to Christ. Whether we are young or old, our rebellious natures always face the call of God to be submissive, as so clearly expressed by the following Scriptures.

> *Wives, be subject to your own husbands, as to the Lord.*
>
> Ephesians 5:22

> *Husbands, love your wives, just as Christ also loved the Church and gave Himself up for her.*
>
> Ephesians 5:25

> *Children, obey your parents in the Lord ... honour your father and mother....*
>
> Ephesians 6:1-2

> *Slaves, be obedient to those who are your masters according to the flesh, with fear and trembling, in the sincerity of your heart, as to Christ.*
>
> Ephesians 6:5

> *Submit yourselves for the Lord's sake to every human institution, whether to a king as the one in authority...*
>
> First Peter 2:13

> *...Be subject to one another in the fear of Christ.*
>
> Ephesians 5:21
>
> *Obey your leaders, and submit to them; for they keep watch over your souls...*
>
> Hebrews 13:17

The Order of Fellowship

As an assembly comes into divine order, many will find the "spiritual family" relationship difficult to cultivate. The reason is that the bonds of commitment have to be deeper than human blood. To be a spiritually covenanted people, we must become totally committed to one another. It is through frequent and close fellowship that shortcomings and needs will be exposed. We become vulnerable to one another. This is necessary if we are to be healed in areas where we are weak. By this interaction participants become a "new man," a collective corporate whole — not individuals living unto themselves. In time, through patience and much testing, we become conscious that we are truly a body. We discover how much we love each other. A miracle has taken place! Only Christ Himself and our mutual love for Him can unite us — not doctrine or the mechanics of meetings. Many will find this bonding process very difficult because, as weaknesses and needs are exposed, they must honestly and often seek help and forgiveness of one another. Our personal and corporate lives can only be healed in this manner. To make matters worse, it will likely involve people who "rub us the wrong way." Our testimony may sound something like this:

"If only I could be in another group where everyone were like me, I would do much better."

God says in reply, *"Just be patient and let Me do My work in you."*

Iron sharpens iron, so one man sharpens another.

Proverbs 27:17

It requires more than ministry for a church to attain maturity. We can have signs and wonders and good preaching yet not see anything substantial built. We are not held together by ministry or organizational structure, but by the bonds of His life. We are being built to contain Him. There is a unique place for each of us in the body, one that no one else can fill. We will fill that place only by being properly related to those around us in Christ so that we come to see our need for one another
(1 Cor. 12:21-22).

...God has placed the members, each one of them, in the body, just as He desired.

First Corinthians 12:18

The body of Christ is an organism of order! Its strength is not only a function of the "muscles of ministry," but also of the "joints and ligaments" that bind members together in fellowship. Both are necessary if the body is to function properly. Christians who have no place of commitment and who wander from one church to another as "spiritual gypsies" will *not* find the maturity that could be theirs in the body of Christ.

Let us now examine the various ways His life is ministered in an assembly.

Chapter Eight

The Ministry of Life

The first step in building a local expression of Christ's body is to lay a proper foundation. This is the burden of the master builders, men who understand the order or pattern by which the Lord's house is constructed. Just because one is a Spirit-filled Christian with an anointing for ministry does not guarantee he has the grace of God to perform such a ministry. Paul says of His ministry:

*According to the **grace** of God which was given to me, as a wise master builder **I laid a foundation** ....*

First Corinthians 3:10

The words "master builder" are translations of two Greek words meaning "beginning craftsman." The first ministry in building a church is to lay a proper foundation.

Every building must have a foundation laid that anticipates the final dimensions and weight of the superstructure to be built upon it. So it is with the Church; without knowledge of *all* that God would build upon it, one cannot lay an adequate foundation. This is why there are "foundation-laying" ministries.

*...You...are of God's household, having been built upon the **foundation of the apostles and prophets**, **Christ Jesus Himself being the corner stone**, in whom the whole building, being fitted together is growing into a holy temple in the Lord; in whom you also are being built together into a dwelling of God in the Spirit.*

Ephesians 2:19-22

Order is needed, both in the timing and the diversity of ministry, to build a spiritual body. Some of Paul's expressions to the Corinthians bear this out:

"I planted, Apollos watered."

"I laid a foundation, and another is building upon it...."

"God has appointed in the Church, first apostles, second prophets, third teachers..."

One reason there is variety in ministry is to ensure that the Church is built with a balance of truth. For example, there are more references in the Bible on *building* the Church than there are on shepherding. Too great an emphasis on shepherding can produce a church of "mothered" saints who are always going to the elders for help with their problems. Strength is missing in their personal relationships to the Lord. Similarly, if there is too great an emphasis on evangelism without adequate teaching and shepherding, there could be a great scattering of new converts to evangelize and little of any consequence built. If there is too great an emphasis on teaching and shepherding without proper evangelism, the church could become ingrown and stagnant. Finally, if there is excellent teaching, shepherding and evangelism but a lack in the prophetic flow, an active church could arise that had no clear vision of the purposes of God for that day. It is this *balance* that apostolic ministries should seek to establish in the church.

It is recorded in Acts 2:42-46 that the early believers met daily from house to house and, in doing so, they continued steadfast in the apostles' teaching, in fellowship, in breaking of bread and in prayer. This is an excellent framework of balance for body ministry. Body ministry is an orchestration of spiritual gifts, worship, and testimony out of hearts that jointly express the mind of the Lord among His people. This harmony of life flow is a living expression of the gospel, for it reveals the love and grace of God in action.

*Now there are **varieties of gifts**, but the same Spirit.
And there are **varieties of ministries**, and the same Lord.
And there are **varieties of effects**, but the same God who
works all things in all persons. But to each one is given the
manifestation of the Spirit for the common good.*

First Corinthians 12:4-7

It is the variety and spontaneity of spiritual manifestations
that are so attractive to those who hunger for more depth in
their relationships to the Lord. Once they experience reality
in the moving of the Spirit in body life, they are forever
spoiled for programed meetings. The diversity and spontaneity
in ministry express the order of His life. Spiritual worship is
also an expression of such order.

*...Worship the Lord in **holy array**.*

Psalm 29:2

How can those with oversight in His house ever bring to
pass this life flow? It is certainly not accomplished by committees, commissions, programs or wishful thinking. The
diakonate must seek to bring His people into this flow of
body life by example and instruction. It is not a question of
interpreting Christ and His ways to the sheep, but of bringing
each one into a personal relationship and union with their
Head from whom life comes. However, it is also not the
confusion of everyone doing their own thing, for in ministry
or worship the elders are responsible to ensure that...

...all things be done properly and in an orderly manner.

First Corinthians 14:40

An "orderly manner" is not a preconceived sequence of
events, but a spontaneous flow of ministry under the government of the Holy Spirit.

*What is the outcome then, brethren? When you
assemble, **each one** has a psalm, has a teaching, has a
revelation, has a tongue, has an interpretation. Let **all***

*things be done for edification. If anyone speaks in a tongue, it should be by two or at the most three, and each in turn, and let one interpret; but if there is no interpreter, let him keep silent in the church; and let him speak to himself and to God. And let two or three prophets speak, and let the others pass judgment. But if a revelation is made to another who is seated, let the first keep silent. For you can all prophesy one by one, so that **all** may learn and **all** may be exhorted; and the spirits of prophets are subject to prophets; for God is not a God of confusion but of peace, as in all the churches of the saints.*

First Corinthians 14:26-33

Some will say, "I don't know the purpose of God in a meeting, so I contribute nothing for fear of being out of order." The answer to this is that the purpose of God is in the Holy Spirit *within us*. If all members honestly seek the Lord's face before a meeting, then His purpose will surely be made known as each one moves in faith. It is true that we must grow into such obedience, since it is easy to confuse human zeal and knowledge with the anointing of the Lord. It is the *diakonate's* responsibility to set examples in these things. The Lord doesn't move in four different directions in a meeting. He has a purpose and direction for each gathering. Learning to flow in a meeting is best taught and entered into in small groups; those who do well here are to be encouraged to minister in the larger meetings.

Each member in a local assembly has a unique ministry and a place to fill for the common good of that body. In the same way, we should expect to see the focus of outreach ministry in different assemblies mature in various directions so there will be a more complete and wholesome testimony overall in a region. An assembly should not seek to become a carbon copy of other assemblies, but should let the Lord develop the particular expression of His life that He desires. For example, local bodies in heavily populated urban areas will likely have a different outreach orientation than those in the countryside (i.e., in evangelism and ministry to the poor). These differences will serve to strengthen the dependency between assemblies and contribute to the overall quality of the church. Traveling ministries will communicate and reinforce these visions and support for them.

Categories of Ministries

Excellence of our personal ministry should *not* be our primary objective; it is but a means to an end. To *know* Christ and to make Him known in the equipping of others is the objective. A Spirit-filled person is one in whom there is a free, unhindered flow of spiritual life. All ministry is to represent the Lord Jesus. If one ministers correct doctrine but does so while living an unholy life, he actually misrepresents the Lord.

> *"He who believes in Me," as the Scripture said, "from his innermost being shall flow rivers of living water."*
>
> John 7:38

This flow of life is ministry. Jesus received the Holy Spirit without measure; however, we receive grace according to the measure of the gift of Christ. That is, we receive a deposit of the Holy Spirit who works to conform each of us into His image, but He also is given individually by measure according to the ministry we have been allotted in Christ. There is a different anointing upon one called to be a deacon than there is upon one called as an apostle. Many skills and crafts are required to build a house; in the same way, many expressions of ministerial life are required to build a church. These can be grouped into three categories.

The first one is made up of the five ascension gift ministries. These can be likened to the "five-fingered hand" of Christ working to lay foundations and equipping the saints.

The five fingers represent the diversity present in these ministries, while the hand itself represents the unity of purpose they have in building the church. These ministries are unique extensions of the body.

> *He who descended is Himself also He who ascended far above all the heavens, that He might **fill all things**. And He gave some as **apostles**, and some as **prophets**, and some as **evangelists**, and some as **pastors and teachers**, for the equipping of the saints for the work of service, to the building up of the body of Christ; until we all attain to the unity of the faith, and of the knowledge of the Son of God, to a mature man, to the measure of the stature which belongs to the fulness of Christ. As a result, we are no longer to be children...but speaking the truth in love, we are **to grow up** in all aspects into Him, who is the head, even Christ.*

Ephesians 4:10-15

Briefly, it may be said that the purpose of these ministries is to equip the saints and see the body of Christ come to maturity. Unity of faith cannot be achieved apart from the input of *all* of these ministries. These ministry graces are what enable elders to oversee and equip the flock of God.

Equipping the saints includes in part impartation of the nine gifts of the Holy Spirit. These gifts represent the second category of ministry (1 Cor. 12 and 14). Spiritual gifts are multi-faceted expressions of the Lord's grace that are offered freely to each member of His body. They are not toys to play with, and they are never intended to honor or exalt the recipients. They are tools by which each member can effectively serve in the building of His house; and each believer may have more than one in his armament. They may be exercised in one-to-one situations as well as being a vital part of life-flow in meetings. As long as we confine our attention to soulish (flesh and blood) realms of activity, we will never see our need for this equipment. However, since our battle is against spiritual forces, our armament *must* also be spiritual.

Three of these gifts are revelatory in nature: the word of wisdom, the word of knowledge, and the discerning of spirits. They provide specific God-given understanding when our human faculties are inadequate. These three are basic essentials in the overall ministry of the diakonate. Three other gifts — prophecy, tongues and the interpretation of tongues — contribute a prophetic content in the flow of the various ministries that involve speech. As such, they often provide signposts to the *diakonate* concerning the direction or purpose the Lord has for His people at the time. The remaining three gifts — the gift of faith, the working of miracles and the gift of healing — while often more demonstrative in nature, are no more important than the others in the spiritual life of an assembly. All gifts are given by the Holy Spirit to equip the whole body for the common good. As a believer, the benefit of your gift is for those with whom you are in fellowship. They serve to teach us our dependency on one another.

> *But one and the same Spirit works **all** these things* [i.e., manifesting the gifts], *distributing to **each** one individually just as He wills.*
>
> First Corinthians 12:11

Spiritual gifts can also play a significant role in evangelism. In whatever assembly spiritual gifts are not considered relevant to church life, the end result is like the body of a full-grown man whose muscles have atrophied; he can accomplish nothing. Many pastors, when moving to a new charge, have found this is exactly what they are inheriting. They have a choice: They may either continue to spoon-feed the invalid or begin to equip the saints for ministry.

The first group represents Christ's gift of certain men whose foundation ministries are given to the whole Church. The second group involves gifts of the Holy Spirit that are offered to all believers: specific gifts to specific individuals distributed for the common good of the assembly. The third category represents various practical ways each believer can release the spiritual life he has in Christ to serve others. Much has been written on the first two classes, so they will not be considered here in detail. Let us examine the third group, which is often not seen as ministry.

Ministries of Relationship

This group I call "ministries of relationship." Like the first two classes, they are diverse and varied, which is in harmony with the order of His life. They represent the many practical, nitty-gritty, person-to-person interactions we go through in our spiritual growth and fellowship together. They can be related to various rungs on the ladder of serving. The value of any truth is realized only when it is received and practiced. We can believe something to be true and yet never possess it as truth in our walk until we act on it. Those interpersonal activities and commitments we must go through to possess truth always involve some ministry of relationship; they are actions that impart life. Let us consider a few of them:

1. *HOSPITALITY*

The early Church was built largely through ministry in homes, while the synagogues were primarily used for evangelism. In the informal atmosphere of a home, people can relate to others more easily. It is here that we begin to see ourselves as others see us. It is a place where honesty can grow and make-believe facades can be removed. Hospitality implies an environment where material things are freely shared with others. The objective of all fellowship is to become more united in Christ in a collective sense. We benefit from the lives of our brothers and sisters in Christ. The strong relationship of the early Church was maintained because the Believers frequently gathered in small groups while going from house to house during the week. It is wonderful to gather in a large assembly and express our identity as one body, but this does not remove the need to come together frequently in small groups. In this context hospitality becomes a vital ministry. When the meeting emphasis is only on large gatherings, there is little likelihood that meaningful relationships will be established between the people. Whether a home is used for a meeting, to provide shelter, or as a place to share food, it can in each case be a place of ministry. The starting point of hospitality is a family household that is properly established in the Lord. It must be a place of peace and order. Priscilla and Aquilla had a church in their home wherever they lived. Hospitality was a key part of their ministry. God extends this same opportunity in some measure to all who have homes. As He leads, we are to use our homes to reach out to others in the body. Prayer meetings in a home show hospitality. Building total lives together is what Church is all about. Something as simple as eating together helps to unite members in one body. To share one's home is to share a personal part of one's life.

2. FRIENDSHIP

Be devoted to one another...

Romans 12:10

Friendship in Christ is not restricted to those we like best or to the more spiritual; indeed, we are to extend our hearts to those who are not really making a go of it; those who don't have it all together. Perhaps it is someone with all sorts of problems or even one who has backslidden. Those in despair often need a friend more than a preacher and would respond more readily to friendship than to a sermon. You may not know how to offer counsel, but you can be a friend. Faith and trust are required in a ministry of friendship. Abraham believed God, and God called him His friend. Be sincere and establish trust with those who open their hearts and confide in you; they are trusting part of their lives to you.

No longer do I call you slaves, for the slave does not know what his master is doing; but I have called you friends, for all things that I have heard from My Father I have made known to you.

John 15:15

Generally, if we trust someone enough to confide in him, we consider that person a friend. We should be available when needed and have an open heart to those we befriend. The road is never long to a friend's house. If you are walking closely with God, your friends can sense this in you and be helped toward a relationship with the Lord through your friendship.

The following Scripture passage gives us a picture of two different kinds of friends.

....Suppose one of you shall have a friend, and shall go to him at midnight, and say to him, "Friend, lend me three loaves; for a friend of mine has come to me from a journey, and I have nothing to set before him"; and from inside he shall answer and say, "Do not bother me; the door has already been shut and my children and I are in bed; I cannot get up and give you anything." I tell you, even though he will not get up and give him anything because he is his friend, yet because of his persistence he will get up and give him as much as he needs.

Luke 11:5-8

This particular person was a friend to one who came asking for bread. However, he didn't have any bread. Because he was a true friend, he said, "I'll go to my other friend, and get some from him." But the second friend replied, "Hey, don't bother me — the children and I are in bed, it is cold, and I'm just not going to get up." However, the real friend was persistent, and finally the man did get up and give him bread, which was then taken back to his visitor. This is a picture of true friendship. The second friend did not contribute much in relationship, even though he did supply the bread. We should be aware that friendship doesn't mean we will always like the person concerned, but we are to be constrained by the love of Christ. There may be many reasons why you would rather not do what is required; but if you are a *true* friend, you *will* go and get bread. Often the important thing is just to be present when needed, being careful not to gossip, lecture or criticize, but to listen and give encouragement. Do this, and you will be seen as a friend, for your concern will be life to him. Gossip or critical words can destroy friendship. If we repeat things, even when they are true, it can bring separation. Therefore, if we are going to be friends, we must learn to keep our mouths closed, our ears open, and our hearts pure. "Opened by mistake" should apply only to our mail, not our mouths!

There is another aspect of friendship:

> *Faithful are the wounds of a friend...*
>
> Proverbs 27:6

To be a true friend, we must at times offer correction. I have friends who have corrected me in the Lord, and it was their sincere concern that proved their friendship to me. Unfortunately, some people would sooner be ruined by praise than redeemed by correction. Friendship is often the key in being able to get a person's attention. A true friend can come on the basis of relationship and expect you to receive correction, even though it may hurt at the time. The Holy Spirit will provide all necessary guidelines in our ministry of friendship as we take time to pray for wisdom. One such guide is knowing when to be present and when to stay away. We can become obnoxious by being around too much; a busybody is often an overzealous, misguided friend. We are to recognize that all problems are intended to draw the party concerned closer to the Lord and, therefore, our friendship must never take the place of the Lord in their lives.

3. SHOWING MERCY

One of the most important ministries of relationship is that of showing mercy, for mercy reflects the nature of God.

...He who shows mercy, with cheerfulness...

Romans 12:8

But if your enemy is hungry, feed him, and if he is thirsty, give him a drink; for in so doing you will heap burning coals upon his head.

Romans 12:20

God gives us opportunities to show mercy, not primarily to our friends, but to strangers, enemies and those who persecute us. Mercy provides a bridge by which relationship can be established between us and those needing Christ. The account in the Scriptures of the Good Samaritan is an excellent example of this ministry (Luke 10:30-37). There is not a single person in the body of Christ who does not have the ministry of mercy, since each one of us became Christians through the mercy of God. Because we have received mercy, God expects us to minister it to others. To be shown mercy is often a first step toward building a relationship with the Lord for those who do not know Him.

Remember the prisoners, as though in prison with them, and those who are ill-treated, since you yourselves also are in the body.

Hebrews 13:3

Why does the Lord say in the Scriptures that He desires mercy more than sacrifice? Well, whatever a sacrifice might cost us to give, it does nothing to establish relationship. However, when you show mercy, you build relationship. When you visit the sick, those in prisons, widows and orphans without considering whether or not they are worthy of your time, you build a bridge of relationship to Christ for them. To those who are hard-hearted, the ministry of mercy can open a door for the Spirit of Christ to touch their lives with the reality of His love.

4. HELPS

*And God has appointed in the church, first apostles, second prophets, third teachers, then miracles, then gifts of healings, **helps**, administrations, various kinds of tongues.*
First Corinthians 12:28

"Helps" is a vital part of every deacon's ministry. Not everyone with the ministry of helps is a deacon, but I believe every deacon has the ministry of helps. Helps is a supporting ministry of the *diakonate* and the entire assembly.

Beloved, you are acting faithfully in whatever you accomplish for the brethren, and especially when they are strangers; and they bear witness to your love before the church;...Therefore we ought to support such men, that we may be fellow workers with the truth.
Third John 5-8

The Lord grant mercy to the house of Onesiphorus for he often refreshed me, and was not ashamed of my chains.
Second Timothy 1:16

Paul's ministry of an apostle was helped by Onesiphorus. "Helps" is one way we share in another's ministry, and we can help others much more than we imagine. For example, we can share the natural things God has given us, such as money, talents, our time, or any service that supports others. Suppose there were five people in the church who could perform all ministry perfectly. Since all needs would be met through these five, everybody else could sit back and do nothing. In that case, there would be very little relationship established in the body. Therefore, God sees to it that individually we are deficient; as others supply us with what He has given them, relationship is established through our need. The eye is not to say to the hand, "I have no need of you"; on the contrary, we are to have confidence in the supply of our brother or sister. God has a purpose when He deposits in us certain skills and latent talents. Giving a glass of cold water is a small thing, but even this can be a step in establishing relationships. The ministry of "helps" is a vital part of *all* life activity in the Church. Women are so often a rich blessing in their roles of "helpers" in the Church.

> *I commend to you our sister Phoebe, who is a servant of the church ... that you help her in whatever matter she may have need of you; for she herself has also been a helper of many, and of myself as well.*
>
> Romans 16:1-2

> *Greet Mary, who has worked hard for you.*
>
> Romans 16:6

> *Indeed, true comrade, I ask you also to help these women who have shared my struggle in the cause of the gospel, together with Clement also, and the rest of my fellow workers, whose names are in the book of life.*
>
> Philippians 4:3

There is a delicate balance of priorities required in the ministry of helps. This is seen in the story of Mary and Martha. Martha was so help-oriented in the horizontal dimension that she neglected her vertical relationship to the Lord. We must not seek service at the cost of our relationship with Him. One New Testament family who practiced a well-balanced ministry of helps was Aquilla and Priscilla (Acts 18:1-3, 18-19, 24-26; 1 Cor. 16:19; Rom. 16:3; 2 Tim. 4:19). They were a consistent help to Paul's ministry; no doubt many relationships of the early Church were established in their home. Whoever aspires to directive ministry in the Church should see "helps" as a valid starting point.

5. BLESSING OTHERS

> *Bless those who persecute you; bless and curse not.*
>
> Romans 12:14

One meaning of the word blessing is "to speak well of." Someone might raise the question: "How are they in the Lord;

do they really obey Him? If they do, then I can speak well of them." But the commandment is to speak well of those who persecute you. It doesn't say to bless only those who are walking with the Lord. God has ordained His people be blessed through His grace. The lesser is blessed by the greater (Heb. 7:7). When we receive blessings from God, He expects us to bless others in turn. That is the principle of blessing. When we see a brother or a sister who is not walking as closely as they should with the Lord, the tendency is to be critical of them. There is a time to correct, but there are also the times when we should bless them. We do not have to honor what they are doing wrong, but we can bless that which is good in their lives to encourage them. For example, we may know a brother who has a problem in his life, but we can say, "Praise the Lord, brother, the testimony you gave the other night really encouraged me." We bless him in that which is good, not pointing to what is lacking.

It is a challenge to bless those who persecute you. However, doing so will lay a foundation on which to build relationships in the future. Jesus called little children to Himself and blessed them. I don't know what really happened, but I suspect a relationship was started that God honored and worked out later in their lives. A primary purpose God has in *all* His dealings with us is that in the end He might bless us. These blessings will flow out of the relationship we build with Him. Husbands and wives are committed to each other by their marriage relationship, which will deepen as they bless one another.

> *Not returning evil for evil, or insult for insult, but giving a blessing instead; for you were called for the very purpose that you might inherit a blessing.*
>
> First Peter 3:9

It requires faith to bless someone in whom you see short-comings. We must not put our thumbs on the scale when we weigh the faults of others. It doesn't take faith to speak evil of somebody or even to speak the truth; but it takes faith to bless because blessing looks to the future.

By faith Isaac blessed Jacob and Esau, even regarding things to come.

Hebrews 11:20

6. REJOICING AND WEEPING WITH OTHERS

Rejoice with those who rejoice, and weep with those who weep.

Romans 12:15

This verse speaks of personal involvement; we are exhorted to identify with the sorrows and joys of others and so build emotional bridges to them (1 Cor. 12:25-26).

We can easily identify with others at an intellectual level, but to rejoice or weep with others we must identify with them out of the depths of our emotions. For example, the richness of another's ministry is something we can and should rejoice in. By doing so, we identify with and support that person. If God uses someone else rather than you in a meeting, don't sulk or be angry because you were not chosen. Encourage that person by rejoicing with him and thereby strengthen your relationship with him. I encourage young Christians who are beginning to move in God to rejoice with one another in the development of their respective ministries so that they will grow to trust each other and learn never to compete with one another.

When I rejoice in the Lord, my whole being participates: I clap my hands, joy is in my heart, and my mind is thinking of good things; everything in me is rejoicing in harmony with the words of my mouth. Members of an assembly should rejoice together in the same manner. When saints gather together, the first objective is *always* to rejoice in the Lord. Some may say, "That sounds good, but I really don't know

what I can rejoice in today; I have nothing but problems."
Well, we rejoice in the Lord, not in our circumstances.

*Rejoice in the Lord **always**; again I will say, rejoice!*
Philippians 4:4

If I can rejoice in Him throughout the week, then it is easy
to rejoice with the assembly. We should *never* be without a
spirit of rejoicing and thankfulness. Joy cannot be saved; it
can only be used up.

In like manner we are to weep with one another. What
happens when you go to someone who is in sorrow and pour
out your heart in comfort and sympathy, weeping with them?
Confidence and relationship are established. As a result, bonds
of love in the body are strengthened. When great sorrow
arises in someone's life from an event that seems to spell
defeat, it is an opportunity for others to help bear their burden.

*Now we who are strong ought to bear the weaknesses
of those without strength and not just please ourselves. Let
each of us please his neighbor for his good, to his edification. For even Christ did not please Himself; but as it is
written, "The reproaches of those who reproached Thee
fell upon Me".*

Romans 15:1-3

One thing that will hinder any depth in this kind of relationship is pride. We can be proud and not realize it; when we are
too timid to speak or too afraid to show our emotions, it can
be pride that hinders us. We may say we are too shy or
humble, but it is often pride that prevents us from opening
our heart and becoming close enough to others to share their
joys and sorrow.

7. COMFORTING OTHERS

*Blessed be the God and Father of our Lord Jesus
Christ, the Father of mercies and God of all comfort; who
comforts us in all our affliction so that we may be able to*

comfort those who are in any affliction with the comfort with which we ourselves are comforted by God.

Second Corinthians 1:3-4

The Holy Spirit is our Comforter. We reflect His nature and ministry when we comfort others. To do so effectively, we must be prepared to undergo trials and problems in order to experience the comfort of God. Through this we learn how to comfort others. When we embrace our problems and distresses, we find they do a work in our hearts that becomes the means of ministering comfort to others. We cannot give something we do not possess ourselves. Only if we have experienced the lifting of a heavy burden in our own lives by the Lord are we likely to be constrained through compassion to bear the burden of others.

8. A PEACEMAKER.

One of the most precious ministries for establishing relationship is that of a peacemaker. We may think a peacemaker is one who comes between warring parties and stops the fighting. We equate God's peace to an armistice, which is not the case. Peace is not a passive absence of war, but active government by Him in our lives. There is peace wherever He governs. His kingdom is joy, peace and righteousness within us. One *cannot* legislate peace.

Blessed are the peacemakers, for they shall be called sons of God.

Matthew 5:9

God is a peacemaker, for He sent His Son to reconcile men to Himself. We are to be like Him and pursue peace with all men. When an open rift exists between brothers, there can arise a root of bitterness that will defile others. The role of peacemaking is to bring each heart into submission to the Lord who is the Prince of Peace. Anyone in the Church can have a ministry of peace *if* his life is under the government of Christ. A child can be a peacemaker at home, just as a parent can be a peacemaker between children. The first target in the Church the enemy seeks to attack is leadership; he attempts to divide the responsible brethren so they are unable to function as one. True collegiality in an eldership can only exist within the peace of God. It requires each man to lay down his right to walk independently and to serve together as one under the government of Christ. Each one must be a peacemaker. Plurality without peace creates confusion. Therefore, pray for your leaders and be at peace among yourselves.

> *And the seed whose fruit is righteousness is sown in peace by those who make peace.*
>
> James 3:18

Many of the circumstances Christians face in their lives are sent to deal with their rebellious natures in order to develop gentleness, reasonableness and mercy. When we attempt to bring peace without these virtues, all we do is meddle; our spirits must be groomed with peace.

9. GIVING ENCOURAGEMENT (EXHORTATION)

> *But encourage one another day after day...*
>
> Hebrews 3:13

We strengthen relationships whenever we exhort and encourage each other in the Lord. Not everyone is a pastor or teacher, but every member of Christ can speak the Word of God to edify others. All may have a spirit of prophecy (which is the testimony of Jesus Christ), even though only a few will have the gift of prophecy and fewer yet are prophets. In the same way there will be degrees of exhortation. At first you may only share a verse of the Scriptures or a simple testimony of what God has done for you. As you grow in Christ, the word you bring will become more substantial. In time, you will give directive exhortation as your word becomes more specific than general. The Lord can lead you to bring forth specifically what is needed in certain lives. Your word of exhortation will help build relationships. It will be a supplement to the teaching ministry of the church. It is vital to keep such a ministry as exhortation and not attempt to make it preaching. One can only minister according to his measure of faith. Exhortation can, in time, grow into a public ministry of the word, but this must come from the anointing of God.

But having the same spirit of faith, according to what is written, "I believed, therefore I spoke," we also believe, therefore also we speak.

Second Corinthians 4:13

If you have faith to do so, exhort on the promises that God reveals to you. Speaking truth is one step toward possession; you hear, you believe, you confess, and you begin to possess. Confession always precedes possession. Relationships can be built if we are faithful to speak the word God gives us. If I have a personal need and God quickens a verse of Scripture to you that truly helps me, I will develop confidence in you since God has used you in my life.

The spirit of suicide is common today and, as greater pressures materialize, I believe it will increase among those without God. To encourage one in despair means, above all else, to give him hope; not hope in himself, but in the Lord. "Hope thou in God" is the message. It is too dark in the well of despair for people to see their faults; they must be encouraged to look up to the light and see His hand reaching down to them. Words of hope can provide a rope of relationship to them.

10. *PERFERRING OTHERS BEFORE OURSELVES*

We honor others when we show them preference over ourselves. This requires humility. Just as water flows downhill, so God's river of anointing flows down upon the lowly and humble.

Be devoted to one another in brotherly love; give preference to one another in honor.

Romans 12:10

Pride of any kind hinders our fellowship with others. Ministries of relationship can only be effective when heart attitudes are right between parties, and humility is the place to start.

Do nothing from selfishness or empty conceit, but with humility of mind let each of you regard one another as more important than himself.

Philippians 2:3

...All of you, clothe yourselves with humility toward one another, for God is opposed to the proud, but gives grace to the humble. Humble yourselves, therefore, under the might hand of God, that He may exalt you at the proper time.

First Peter 5:5-6

We are to humble ourselves under God and submit to one another, not only in meetings but also in the sphere of practical activities where our lives touch during the week. Honoring others is essential in serving them. Our whole life can be a ministry when we prefer brothers and sisters before ourselves, not only in spiritual affairs but also through the grace of common courtesy in our everyday lives.

We do not develop fruits of the Spirit for our personal use, for we are to release these virtues in ministries of life to others. We are the extension of His life on earth. As life is ministered in our relationships to one another, changes take place. Tolerance becomes love, pity becomes compassion, curiosity becomes concern, gossip becomes prayer, self-pity becomes repentance, insecurity becomes confidence, problems become blessings and, best of all, defeats become victories.

What we are taught through the fivefold ministries and receive from the ministry of spiritual gifts we are to practice in ministries of relationship. This is how the stones are shaped and fitted together in the Lord's house.

We will next examine the pattern for building His house.

Chapter Nine

The Pattern of His House

We Need a Blueprint

A pile of stones is not a house. Each stone must be shaped to fit into the one spot designed for it. Thus, there is a pattern both for the fashioning and finishing of each stone as well as to where individual stones are to be located in the structure of the house. The same principle holds true for those who build a church. They have no right to build lives together any way they please. We would never assemble the materials for a house and then start nailing things together without following a blueprint. Most of us have seen children construct playhouses in this manner; they were great to play in but not suitable to live in. We do not have the right to lead people to Christ and then organize some arbitrary structure we have devised in our minds or copied from religious tradition. The pattern of His house is given in the Scriptures. We are to search out and follow the pattern of maturity in Christ and the pattern by which He is building us together as living stones in His house.

The phrase "a New Testament Church" is often heard today and, though I don't care for this expression, I use it myself in the absence of anything better to speak of a spiritually sound local expression of the body of Christ. The Lord is *not* restoring the Church to the level attained by early-Christians; He is building it to a level of maturity and glory never seen before. However, this will be done using the pattern and principles of the early Church. Therefore, our vision must be oriented both to the *pattern of the past* as well as to the *goal of the future*.

First, the Natural

It has been said that the Old Testament is the New concealed and the New Testament is the Old revealed. This involves a spiritual principle, one that Paul presents in his exposition on resurrection:

However, the spiritual is not first, but the natural; then the spiritual.

First Corinthians 15:46

The Lord began to reveal His ways and purposes for man by using examples of natural things. For example, in the material and characteristics of the Old Testament tabernacle He established patterns and types that were prophetic in foretelling His ultimate intention for the Church. His purpose, like His person, is the same yesterday, today and forever, so that the record of His relationship with Israel in the past contains the promises of our destiny. His instructions for our future are best understood in the light of all He has already spoken. That which is yet to be manifest in and to the Church is hidden in the Scriptures.

For this reason we need not be ignorantly passive concerning what is to come, i.e., "I am saved, so I will just wait, and whatever is to happen will happen." Instead, we are to exercise faith in the promises of God, seek out His will for our lives and fulfill it.

We cannot hope to succeed without having a clear, balanced understanding of the current redemptive works of the Holy Spirit and the Lord's plan for His Church through the events that are coming to pass in the earth. We are living in troubled times and days of transition, but we are also living in a time of restoration, a period when much religious tradition is being discarded. There is a sweetness in our mouths as we fed on the word of revelation. Because we are walking a pathway on which there are fewer and fewer footsteps, it is mandatory that we be sure of our steps. The pattern of our personal and corporate redemption as shown in the tabernacle is a road map to guide our walk.

The following are some materials and physical character-istics of the tabernacle that help explain spiritual truths. Each is listed with its spiritual counterpart. In order to recognize the significance associated with the tabernacle structure and the priesthood functions, it is necessary to understand that certain materials and physical characteristics were used as types or shadows of spiritual truths. This is similar to the principle Jesus used in His parables. The following are examples of these types:

1. Oil — the Holy Spirit (Matt. 25:38; James 5:14)
2. White linen — righteousness (Rev. 19:8)
3. Water — the Scriptures (Eph. 5:26; John 15:3)
4. Silver — redemption (Matt. 26:15; Exod. 30:12-16)
5. Purple — royalty (John 19:1-5)
6. Blue — obedience (Num. 15:38-40)
7. Wood — human nature (Is. 61:3; Judg. 9:10-15; Matt. 7:15-20; Ezek. 17:22-24; Is. 55:12-13)
8. Gold — divine nature (Rev. 3:18; Song of Sol. 5:10-15; Rev. 14:14)
9. Scarlet — blood of Christ (Josh. 2:18-21; 6:25; Heb. 9:12-23)

His House in Israel
The tabernacle that Moses built was God's house during the period of His covenant with Israel. It was patterned after the heavenly sanctuary (Heb. 8:2-5; 9:11, 23-34) and pre-figures the house the Lord is building today in His Church.

*Now Moses was faithful in all His house as a servant, for a testimony of those things **which were to be spoken later**; but Christ was faithful as a Son over His house, **whose house we are**...*

Hebrews 3:5-6

Thus the pattern of the Church has its origin in heaven. Although we may not understand it, what is being built on earth, in and between local assemblies, is to reflect the order of what is built above, which will also one day exist as the city of God on earth (Gal. 4:26-27; Rev. 21:9-10; John 14:2-3). The first physical manifestation of how God dwells with men is revealed in the tabernacle of Moses. For this reason, the Lord instructed Moses with great emphasis to be sure to build it according to the pattern He gave him on the mountain (Ex. 25:9, 40; 26:30; 27:8). If we are walking with our gaze on the ground and approach a building, the first view we have of it is its shadow. This portrays only relative dimensions and outline of the building and does not reveal any substance or detail. The tabernacle was in this sense a shadow of the Church. Indeed, this was its primary purpose. The Lord told Moses why the tabernacle was to be built:

> *And let them construct a sanctuary for Me, that I may dwell among them.*

> Exodus 25:8

It is quite amazing to see how mankind has always focused on church buildings, where they suppose He is present and how man thinks He is to be worshiped. Christians are so often concerned that it be proper and correct, as though He would be less than He is if some furniture were lacking or out of place. It appears that in our humanity we can better relate to where God may be found than we can to what He is like. In other words, as long as He is supposedly in the consecrated place of worship where we meet, then everything must be all right. However, God's house is made of people, not bricks and stone. At no time has He sought to live in physical buildings other than to teach us of His ways, as in the tabernacle.

> *However, the Most High does **not** dwell in houses made by human hands.*

> Acts 7:48

The house in which God will abide forever is the one He Himself is building in the Spirit: the place of His rest, a place of eternal supply and joy (Ps. 132:13-17). It cannot be organized by man; it must be built by God. He is the Architect, the

Foundation and the Builder; it is His life in men that is the material, and His glory will someday fill it.

Building Material

The material used in construction (gold, silver, precious stones and cloth) originated in Egypt when Israel plundered the Egyptians during the exodus (Ex. 12:35-36). It is the same today: the most precious stones in the Church are often those saints who were the deepest of sinners in the world. The Lord plunders the world to build His house. He uses material man discards such as warped boards and bent nails. It is not our backgrounds that qualify us as material for the Church, but what He builds into us of Himself.

The only Israelites who participated in building the tabernacle were those with a willing spirit, those whose hearts stirred them to freely bring their contributions and skills. From among these, the Lord anointed certain ones with specific abilities to perform the various skilled tasks as required (Ex. 35:5-35). We are co-workers with Christ on the same basis. We must freely give ourselves to Him; that is all He asks. Our place and function will arise out of the anointing of His Spirit on us. We do not educate ourselves to minister; we simply offer ourselves to Him. We minister out of the anointing of the Holy Spirit; the character of His life built within us is the qualification of that ministry.

The Entrance of His House

Let us imagine a person wandering around in the wilderness seeking the presence (or house) of God during the time of the tabernacle. The first thing he eventually sees are walls of white linen, supported on wooden pillars surrounding an area of 150 feet by 75 feet (Ex. 27:9-15). White linen speaks of the righteous acts of the saints. This is what the world should first see as evidence of God's presence in the Church: not buildings, programs or organizations, but the righteous life of Christ being lived in His people. This is the Bible read by the world; it is easily understood and it points everyone to Christ.

Let your light shine before men in such a way that they may see your good works, and glorify your Father who is in heaven.

Matthew 5:15

As our seeker walks around these walls he will come to a thirty-foot-wide gate leading into the tabernacle on the side facing east. This gate was a curtain of purple, blue and scarlet-colored material supported by four wooden pillars (Ex. 27:16). It is the gateway to His house. The significance of this entrance is seen in the colors. They speak of a door that is provided by a king (purple), who was obedient (blue), and who shed His blood (scarlet). This is King Jesus! The door is supported, or presented, to those who would enter by four wooden pillars. Since wood is a type of humanity, these four wooden pillars speak to us of the four men — Matthew, Mark, Luke and John — who wrote the gospels that present Jesus as the way of salvation. A hanging curtain requires no special key or human strength to open. One needs only lean against it to enter. This fact, plus the great width of the entrance, tells us that it is by abundant grace that we are saved and not by our own works or ability. This gate is the only entrance and the first step we all must take if we are to be accepted into the presence of God. Jesus said:

I am the door; if anyone enters through Me, he shall be saved...

John 10:9

Cross

Before us are all the items that pertain to our growth in Christ. The furniture in the tabernacle, the three gates, and the articles in the court are positioned so as to form a cross, with the curtain through which we have come through being the bottom of that cross. Each item speaks to us of a vital part of our growth process and as such is arranged in the necessary sequence to instruct and encourage us in the various phases of our maturity. Just as there are nine spiritual gifts and nine spiritual fruits, so there are nine items that constitute this cross of maturity. Let us walk up the cross, considering each item as we go.

Having passed through this first curtain, we find ourselves facing a copper-covered wood altar that is between six and seven feet square and approximately four and one-half feet high (Ex. 27:1-8). This was the largest object in the outer court or in the tabernacle. Its prominent size speaks of the importance of sacrifice. Once we are saved, the first step required of us is to present our bodies as a living sacrifice to Christ. This is the key to any future growth; we don't mature only by receiving His life, we must lay down our lives as well.

> *I urge you therefore, brethren, by the mercies of God,
> to **present your bodies a living** and holy **sacrifice,** acceptable
> to God...*

> Romans 12:1

This involves two initial steps for the new believer: becoming united with Him in the likeness of His death through water baptism, and being baptized in the Holy Spirit, who is the fire of God. This altar was continually used by the priests to offer sacrifices for sin; we too must continually present ourselves as a sacrifice to avoid going our own way. The animals were tied to the four horns of the altar so they could not escape. For us there are four voluntary constraints that we embrace as commitments to remain in a place of sacrifice:

1. Commitment to His lordship, and thus to His word.
2. Faith and trust in the dealings He brings into our lives (even when we don't understand them).
3. Commitment to those over us in the Lord.
4. Commitment to those we serve in Christ.

As we walk beyond the altar toward the tabernacle, we come next to a laver filled with water. This laver was made of polished copper taken from the women's mirrors. The priests were required to wash their hands and feet here before they could enter the tabernacle to minister (Ex. 30:18-21; 38:8). Before we can be a holy priesthood unto Him or become a mature, spotless Church, we must be a people who continually wash ourselves in the Word of God. We cannot minister as priests if we recognize iniquity to be in our hearts.

That He might sanctify her, having cleansed her by the washing of water with the word, that He might present to Himself the Church in all her glory, having no spot or wrinkle...

Ephesians 5:26-27

To be washed by the Word involves two things: understanding and obedience. Understanding is vital, since to be cleansed requires that we first see our need and understand the remedy. This will not happen until our understanding is opened by the Scriptures, enabling us to judge the thoughts and intents of our hearts (Heb. 4:12). The laver was made of mirrors; and the Word is precisely that to those who search it in sincerity. We begin to see ourselves in the same way the Lord sees us. Once our character is exposed to us by the mirror of the Scriptures, we are constrained to put off what is unclean. Moreover, the Word, as a mirror, also reflects those changes that occur in us as we are cleansed. We begin to reflect Him little by little as the Holy Spirit unfolds our needs, enabling us to change and put on the Lord Jesus Christ.

But we all, with unveiled face beholding as in a mirror the glory of the Lord, are being transformed into the same image from glory to glory....

Second Corinthians 3:18

The key is revelation; we are not cleansed by following rules and laws of conduct. We must have our need revealed and be obedient to what we are shown. We walk according to the law of the Spirit of life in Christ Jesus. This is a continuing process, for we will always see new needs after we deal with those we already know.

The entrance, the altar and the laver primarily foreshadowed our relationship to Christ. As we enter into the tabernacle proper, we now face not only greater commitments in our personal lives, but also in the area of our covenant relationship with other members of the body of Christ. To possess these new truths, we must continue to experience cleansing at the laver. If our hearts are not prepared to embrace new truth, we will only acquire head knowledge that will not be worked out as truth in our lives. This is why the laver is positioned just prior to the entrance to the tabernacle and why the priests had to wash there *every* time they entered the Holy Place. We cannot neglect washing ourselves in the Word if we expect to flow in what God is doing today in the Church.

The tabernacle was actually made up of two "rooms" or tents; the larger, outer one called the Holy Place and the inner one (which contained the top of the cross we are considering) called the Holy of Holies (Heb. 9:1-7). The entrance into the Holy Place was a curtain similar in appearance to the one leading into the outer court, except it was higher and more narrow. The material was fine linen colored purple, blue and scarlet. This curtain speaks of Christ being presented as the Way into the Holy Place and, therefore, into whatever truth is contained or represented there. However, this curtain was supported by five wooden pillars, each of which was covered with gold (Ex. 26:36-37). These pillars again refer to men, so that the entrance, in this instance, speaks of entering into those truths of Christ ministered by the five ascension gift ministries: apostles, prophets, evangelists, pastors and teachers. The gold which covered the wood of the pillars encourages us not to focus on the humanity of such ministries, but to recognize that they are love gifts of Christ to the Church and He should be seen in them.

As we enter the Holy Place, we see before us two pieces of furniture, one on the left and one on the right. These represent, by their position, the horizontal member of the cross. The piece on our left, to the south, is a beautiful golden lampstand (Ex. 25:31-40). This provided the only light by which the priests could minister, for there were no windows in the Holy Place. It consisted of a central lamp stem with three branches on either side, so that the lampstand had a total of seven branches, or seven lamps. Although the lampstand was very ornate, it was hammered out of one piece of solid gold. The lamp was fueled by pure olive oil. Since the lamp is made of gold, it must refer to God; the oil speaks of the Holy Spirit, and light from the lamp denotes revelation. We can better understand the significance of these things if we examine certain Scriptures concerning the sanctuary in heaven.

> *Grace to you and peace, from Him who is and who was and who is to come; and from the **seven** Spirits of God.*
>
> Revelation 1:4

> *And there were **seven** lamps of fire burning before the throne, which are the **seven** Spirits of God.*
>
> Revelation 4:5

> *And I saw between the throne...and the elders a Lamb standing, as if slain, having **seven** horns and **seven** eyes, which are the **seven** Spirits of God, sent out into all the earth.*
>
> Revelvation 5:6

We know there is only one Spirit of God; the seven eyes, the seven lamps and seven Spirits speak of seven characteristics of His person that God has chosen to reveal by the Spirit to His people. These are basic truths we can all experience in our relationship with Him. Each trait was first revealed to Israel, and each expressed a promise of His personal supply for His people. These seven attributes, each of which was personally confirmed by Christ in His ministry, are listed as follows:

1. *Jehovah-Shalom* — "The Lord is (our) peace." The Lord revealed to Gideon that, despite His awesome magnificence, He was a God of peace to His people (Judg. 6:21-24). When Jesus came, it was as the Prince of Peace, and the Way of Peace (Eph. 2:14-17; Rom. 5:1; Col. 3:15). Can you imagine your relationship to the Lord if He weren't your peace? This is basic in our union with Him. The Lord of Peace Himself continually grants us peace in every circumstance.

2. *Jehovah-Nissi* — "The Lord is our banner or victor." The Lord revealed Himself as the Victor of Israel to Moses in the battle against the Amalekites (Ex. 17:8-15). Jesus overcame the powers of darkness for us. He is our Victor; we can do all things through Him. Indeed, we can only conquer through Him (Phil. 4:13; 1 Cor. 15:57; 2 Cor. 2:14). We are strong in the power of His might. Our triumph is in Him!

3. *Jehovah-Jireh* — "The Lord will provide." When God supplied the ram in the thicket for Abraham's sacrifice, He revealed Himself as the God who provides for His children (Gen. 22:13-14). This revelation of the Lord is not only confirmed in Christ by many New Testament Scriptures, but also by numerous experiences of each one of us. The riches of heaven are ours through Him.

And my God shall supply all your needs according to His riches in glory in Christ Jesus.

Philippians 4:19

We can agree with James that every good thing bestowed and every perfect gift comes down from our Father above (James 1:17); He is our Provider indeed!

4. *Jehovah-Shammah* — "The Lord is present." When the Lord described to Ezekiel the future city in which He will one day dwell among His people, He named it "Jehovah-Shammah." It is a wonderful truth that God is not isolated in some geographic location in heaven; He lives with and in His people. Jesus said:

I will never desert you, nor will I ever forsake you.

Hebrews 13:5

...and lo, I am with you always, even to the end of the age.

Matthew 28:20

How can we walk in victory or into a new circumstance without knowing that His presence is always with us?

5. *Jehovah-Rapha* — "The Lord our healer." The Lord tested Israel at Marah, where He made the bitter waters sweet. He charged them through Moses that if they would obey Him and keep His statutes, He would put none of the diseases on them that He had put on the Egyptians, for He was "the Lord their healer" (Ex. 15:26). This truth was confirmed dramatically by the Lord Jesus' ministry as He healed the sick and commissioned His twelve disciples to do likewise. He continues to manifest Himself in this way today through the gifts of healing and prayer of faith for the sick (1 Cor. 12:9; James 5:14-15). His stripes prove this truth to us.

6. *Jehovah-Raah* — "The Lord my Shepherd." Perhaps more than any other expression of His relationship to Israel, the Lord was best known as their Shepherd (Ps. 23:1; Ps. 80:1; Is. 40:11; Jer. 31:10; Ezek. 34:12, 23-24). This was also the primary focus of Jesus in establishing the identity of His ministry to His people (John 10:1-27).

I am the good shepherd; the good shepherd lays down His life for the sheep.

John 10:11

The Lord's role as our shepherd is clarified when we recognize how sheep so clearly exemplify our needs and limitations; we are prone to go our own way, to scatter from one another and expose ourselves to dangers. Without Jesus, the great Shepherd of the sheep, we would be scattered in the earth.

7. *Jehovah-Tsidkenu* — "The Lord our righteousness." The primary lamp of the candlestick was located on the center

stem of the lampstand; it was from this shaft that the other six branches emerged with their lamps. In the same way, it is only when we know the Lord as our righteousness that we can appropriate and know Him in the other six ways He has chosen to reveal Himself. It was Jeremiah who first prophesied of Him as "the Lord our righteousness" (Jer. 23:5-6); this, more than anything else, is the central theme of the New Testament; all else flows out of this truth (Rom. 3:21-26; 5:19; 10:3-10; 1 Cor. 1:30). It is only in and through Him that we are able to understand righteousness, and only by His life can we become a righteous people (2 Cor. 5:21).

We need to personally possess each of these seven revelations of the Lord in order to appropiate the fulness of His promises. Not to do so is to walk with a corresponding leanness in our souls.

The right arm of the cross is represented by a table located to our right on the north side of the holy place. Upon this table rested twelve loaves of bread. The table was made of wood covered with pure gold with a gold crown or border around its upper surface. The bread was called the "bread of (His) Presence"; it was always present; it was eaten by the Aaronic priesthood and replaced fresh every sabbath. The twelve loaves represented the entire nation, one loaf for each tribe (Ex. 25:23-30; Lev. 24:5-9). There were also bowls located at the table to be used for the libations or drink offerings. A libation involved the priests pouring out wine before the Lord at the doorway of the tent as part of various offerings and sacrifices (Ex. 29:40-43; Num. 28:7-31). Implicit in this piece of furniture is a clear picture of the Lord's table from which we eat and drink in the Church. The communion service is not the "table of the Church," it is the Lord's table, and *no* true believer should be excluded from partaking. The twelve loaves signify that His body was broken for *each* of the twelve tribes of Israel, and they also speak of His presence today in the communion bread for *all* believers. The wine libations represent the pouring out of His blood of the new covenant. The many offerings of wine (drink offerings) and the continual eating of the bread of His presence by the priests speak of our need as His priests today to feed on Him. The communion service is a covenant meal. It is a proclamation to the world above, around and beneath us of the blood covenant relationship we jointly have with Christ (1 Cor. 10:16-17). It is *absolutely* basic to the unity of believers; to speak of Christian unity without a common table is a travesty of truth! There is no place in the Lord's heart for a spirit of exclusivity or elitism concerning His children; and there cannot be any in our hearts either.

Standing between the candlestick and the table directly before us is the altar of incense, the tallest article of furniture in the tabernacle. It was made of wood and covered with gold. Fragrant incense was burned unto the Lord morning and night by Aaron when he trimmed the lights of the lamp-stand (Ex. 30:1-10). The sweet-smelling incense is a type of the worship, praise, and prayer we offer up as His priests today. The height of this altar speaks of its importance; there is *no* greater ministry than worshiping the Lord in spirit and in truth. This is the *primary* ministry of His house. Our worship and prayers rise to the altar of the sanctuary in heaven (Rev. 8:3-4a). They are never to cease.

> *You also, as living stones,* **are being built up** *as a spiritual house for a holy priesthood,* **to offer up** *spiritual sacrifices acceptable to God through Jesus Christ.*
>
> First Peter 2:5

The fire that burned incense on this altar was taken from the fire on the great altar at the entrance to the outer court. This speaks of the sincerity we must have to worship in spirit and in truth; it is to be a result of having already offered ourselves to Him, so that what comes forth in worship is a natural flow from the commitment of our hearts, not merely sounds from our mouths. The blood of the sin offering was poured on the horns of this altar once a year for the annual atonement of sin in Israel. Prayer and worship are rooted in appreciation and love for what He has done in washing our sins away and making us acceptable in His presence. Worship is the incense of redemption (Rev. 5:8-14). I cannot imagine a mature Christian who does not have a desire to pray and worship. The incense was made of equal parts of four spices: red (stacte), black (onycha), brown or yellow (galbanum) and white (frankincense). This speaks of the Lord's desire for communion with every race and color of man (Ex. 30:34-38).

The Presence of God

Immediately beyond this altar was another curtain which was the entrance into the Holy of Holies. This curtain was similar in appearance and size to the entrance into the Holy Place, but was suspended on four wooden pillars overlaid with gold (Ex. 26:31-33). This was the curtain which was ripped from top to bottom when Christ was crucified, thus signifying that the breaking of Christ's body on the cross opened the way for all to come into the presence of God (Matt. 27:50-51). Prior to Calvary only the high priest was allowed to enter the Holy of Holies, where God was present above the mercy seat. Although these four wooden pillars signify the presentation of the message of Christ in the four gospels, its position in the cross we are considering indicates that this curtain represents more than just coming for initial salvation. For example, the beatitudes become more vital and real to us as we mature. The more we grow in our knowledge of Him, the more we understand the great need for coming frequently to the throne of grace. This entrance was not as wide as the outer gate, and speaks of a narrower way; it is a call to come into His presence, to learn of Him and find mercy and grace. We are to come with repentance and in faith, not only as individuals but as a people. We cannot grow personally or corporately apart from the abundant supply of His mercy and grace (John 1:16). It is a dangerous thing to have no sense of need for these virtues; we *always* need grace and mercy, and we see our need more clearly the more we grow in Him.

> *Let us therefore draw near* **with confidence** *to the throne of grace, that we may receive mercy and may find grace to help in time of need.*
>
> Hebrews 4:16

> *Since therefore, brethren,* **we have confidence** *to enter the holy place by the blood of Jesus, by a new and living way which He inaugurated for us through the veil, that is His flesh...***let us draw near with a sincere heart in full assurance of faith,** *having our hearts sprinkled clean from an evil conscience and our bodies washed with pure water. Let us hold fast the confession of our hope without wavering...and let us consider how to stimulate one another to love and good deeds, not forsaking our own assembling together....*
>
> Hebrews 10:19-25

I have observed that new or immature Christians generally speak mostly of their conversion experiences, whereas those who manifest real growth are concerned with what Christ is currently doing in their lives. For such Christians, the altar of incense and the curtain into the Holy of Holies become practical realities of their pressing into God.

The Lord's presence was behind this second curtain, over the mercy seat of the ark. This access to Himself is a primary concern of the Lord in these closing days of salvation. When the ark was returned to Israel by David, he did not put it in the tabernacle which was at Gibeon. There, the Levitical priesthood was busy carrying out their ministry in the tabernacle, despite the fact that the Lord was not present. Instead, David placed the ark in a tent near his house where he could continually enjoy the presence of God and bless the people of

Israel (1 Chron. 16:1-40). David's attitude of seeking the presence of God is what the Lord desires to restore to all men. This is the heart call of the Spirit today (Rev. 22:17). His presence is not always where the religious activity is greatest, but He is always near us behind the rent veil.

> *After these things I will return, and I will rebuild the tabernacle of David which has fallen, and I will rebuild its ruins, and I will restore it, in order that the rest of mankind may seek the Lord...*

Acts 15:16-17

We come to the end of our journey "up the cross" when we stand before the ninth item, the ark of the covenant inside the Holy of Holies (Ex. 25:10-22). The ark was a wooden box overlaid with gold inside and outside; above it was a pure gold mercy seat, having two golden cherubim with spread wings facing inward toward each other from the two ends of the mercy seat. It was here that God dwelt. Let us examine these objects to understand why they speak of the maturity to which we are called. The Lord instructed Moses to place the following three things in the ark as a testimony (Heb. 9:4).

The first of these was manna (Ex. 16:14-15, 31-35). A jar (one omer) of manna was to be a perpetual testimony of how we are to derive our spiritual food. Jesus is the living Bread, the Bread of God that we must "gather daily" to feed our souls. The manna gathered was shared with others so that all had sufficient. It is the same in the body of Christ; we are to share the Bread of Life with other members. What was "gathered" today does not suffice for tomorrow; we must have living bread *every day*. Our bread is to do His will, to eat His word and to partake of His body and blood as one people. Jesus said:

> *...I live because of the Father, so he who eats Me, he also shall live because of Me.*

John 6:57

The two stones upon which the Ten Commandments were inscribed were placed in the ark to remind Israel of the law of God and reveal to them the state of their own hearts. This clearly speaks to us of having the law of the Spirit written on our hearts.

> *...I will put My law within them, and on their heart I will write it; and I will be their God, and they shall by My people.*

> Jeremiah 31:33

Maturity is not knowing right from wrong based on what is written in stone, but rather based on what the Spirit of God has inscribed in our hearts. This is the law of the Spirit of life in Christ Jesus, which sets us free from written laws if we obey His promptings (Rom. 8:2).

The third item of the testimony was Aaron's rod. The authority of Aaron's priesthood was established before Israel by God during a time of rebellion (Num. 17; 18:1-8). Each tribe was told to place a rod in the sanctuary overnight. The next morning, Aaron's rod for the tribe of Levi had sprouted, put forth buds, produced blossoms and bore almonds. By this supernatural sign God demonstrated His selection of Aaron. The authority of men in the *diakonate* must have the same qualifications evident before the people. If we exercise His authority, it is to come from the fragrance of a sweet spirit (blossoms), from one who brings forth new life in others (buds) and has fruits of the Spirit (almonds) in his life. This expresses the gentle authority of servanthood.

The gold-covered wood of the ark signifies one whose humanity is hidden behind the nature of God. When a person has the above testimony of the Lord within him and is one who abides in the presence of God under the blood of the mercy seat, we can say that he is a mature Christian. It is here we can reign with Him, for He is now reigning in our lives!

The cherubim are significant, for they speak of the ministry of angels. The purposes of God are always worked out for man in concert with the ministry of angels.

Are they [angels] *not all ministering spirits, sent out to render service for the sake of those who will inherit salvation?*

Hebrews 1:14

Spiritually every time God began to do a new thing in His relationship with man it was ushered in by a prominent ministry of angels. Some examples include:

- Adam's removal from Eden
- Final promise concerning Isaac (Abrahamic Covenant)
- Beginning of Israel (Genesis 32)
- Exodus of Israel from Egypt
- Birth of John
- Birth of Jesus
- The temptation of Jesus
- The resurrection of Jesus
- The ascension of Jesus
- Ministry in the early Church

For this reason, we can expect to see angels become an increasing part of the spiritual ministry that will unfold in the days ahead as the Lord brings His Church into her fulness. However, we are *not* to command angels in their tasks; we are *not* to pray to them or commit ourselves, or what we possess, into their hands. This is the Lord's responsibility, and we must look to Him alone. To do otherwise leaves us open to great deception.

Growth in the Body of Christ

As we progressed up the cross, we have considered our growth in Christ largely from a personal point of view. Let us go back to the entrance into the holy place, to the curtain supported by five wooden pillars. This represents the doorway into truths concerning the body of Christ. These are the truths revealed through the five-fold ministries that build us together and equip us under the Lord's headship.

This relationship is pictured in the structure of the tabernacle walls (Ex. 26:15-30). The walls were constructed of straight, smooth vertical boards that were fifteen feet high and twenty-seven inches wide. The interesting thing about the wood is that it was cut from the acacia tree. The wood of this tree was very hard, gnarled and close-grained. It required much effort and skill to bring forth smooth, straight boards with surfaces that could be fitted together to make straight walls. This speaks so clearly of our human nature; it is hard and crooked from sin and goes its own way. Our nature resists change. We are well aware of the great dealings God brings into our lives to change and fashion our hearts, so we can be fitted together with brothers and sisters as one body in Christ.

The boards were mounted in a vertical position parallel to one another, all pointing toward heaven; no board was above another; all were in the same position relative to the others. We are all equal before God. Each board was mounted in a tightly coupled fashion to its two neighboring boards. This expresses the truth that in each church believers are to be members of one another, for the strength of an assembly is measured by the strength of their bond of fellowship with one another. We cannot be independent; each of us has been fashioned to fit in the place prepared for us in His body, just as each board was fitted in position. Each board was kept above the dirt of the earthen floor of the tabernacle by being mounted on two sockets of silver. This tells us that His redemption (silver) saves and keeps us from (above) sin. Each board was placed on its sockets and held in position by two extensions called "tenons." The Hebrew word for tenon is *yad*, which means "hand." Thus, each board was held securely in place by two hands. This is a picture of the "laying on of hands" ministry in the church, which serves to identify and confirm the place and ministry of each believer, so that recognition and support by other members enable the whole body to function in unison and harmony (Acts 6:6, 1 Tim. 4:14; 2 Tim. 1:6).

Even though the boards were correctly positioned at their base by the sockets and tenons, because of their great height they required additional support to enable them to jointly form a uniformly straight wall. This was provided by five wooden bars that were mounted in parallel, horizontal positions on the outside surface of the boards. One of these bars, located in the center of each of the three walls, extended along the entire length. These bars represent the five ministries of the Church, that as elders or traveling ministries, equip the saints. The physical strength and stability imparted to the walls by these bars express the spiritual order and stability of an assembly established and shepherded through the graces of these fivefold ministries. Each wall stood as one large board, illustrating how assemblies are to stand as one man. A local body can easily be fragmented and divided without these five bars "holding the wall straight." The significance of the *horizontal* position of the bar is that they *serve* the other boards, indicating that these five ministries are servants of the church. The bar located in the center is the longest, for it touches and supports each board in the entire wall. This expresses the dimension of an apostolic ministry. Since apostles serve as "master builders" or "foundation layers" of assemblies, their vision embraces and touches the total body. They understand how each of the various parts of the body are to fit together and function as a whole.

An apostle's ministry is to build within a certain area or sphere. He is *not* to overextend himself, and he should avoid building on other men's foundations, being conscious of the call of God that sent him forth. Paul speaks of these things in his own ministry.

> *...And thus I aspired to preach...that I might not build upon another man's foundation.*
>
> Romans 15:20

But we will not boast beyond our measure, but within the measure of the sphere which God apportioned to us as a measure, to reach even as far as you. For we are not overextending ourselves...not boasting beyond our measure, that is, in other men's labors, but with the hope that as your faith grows, we shall be, within our sphere, enlarged even more by you.

Second Corinthians 10:13-15

This center bar on the end wall was different in length than those on the side walls, which tells us that apostolic ministries can be different in scope and magnitude. Some will be men called to build within a given locality, others will be anointed to build over a greater geographic area. The Lord is as concerned about the detail of the overall body as He is for the smallest detail in any assembly. Apostles must recognize these dimensions of God-given responsibility in their ministries and *not* attempt to reach beyond the measure of grace they are given.

It is unfortunate that today many "New Testament" churches which have been founded by valid apostolic and supporting ministries often have no fellowship with other churches established by equally valid ministries. Unfortunately, this often arises from nonessential differences in doctrine or methods. To the unsaved, a spirit of disunity is a great hindrance to the testimony of a church. We must walk in the truth that we are *one* body. Unity is not maintained by translocal authority, but by a translocal spirit of submission and serving one another. How this unity can be attained is partly revealed in the manner by which the tabernacle walls were joined together. Even if each wall were straight, the rear wall had also to be perfectly united with the two side walls to form stable, right-angled corners. This was accomplished by two rings, one at the top and one at the bottom, which joined the end boards of the walls and held them tightly together. It requires more than correct doctrine and good ministry to unite bodies of believers; it also requires an overflow of the *peace* and *love* of God, which is what these two rings represent.

> *Being diligent to preserve the unity of the Spirit in the bond of peace.*
>
> Ephesians 4:3

> *And beyond all these things put on love,* which is the perfect *bond* of unity
>
> Colossians 3:14

These two virtues are sufficient to bond together individual, separate assemblies which have been built upon proper foundations. Peace and love *always* provide the basis for unity, since they reflect the presence of Christ's government.

The word "bond" comes from the Greek word *sudesmos* which means "joint bond (or band)." These bonds or rings were not large, but in their absence the walls would simply fall flat. It is not different in the Church. We can have the right organization with all the ministries and yet *fail completely* in the unity we are called to with other bodies if we are not deeply established in the peace and love of God. It is not the "correct structure" of an eldership that marks the government of God in an assembly; it is the peace that flows from the presence of His headship in their midst. For example, an assembly under the oversight of a plural leadership who are not united in love and who rule the flock with heavy-handed dominance cannot produce the peace of His government.

On the other hand, the authority of a godly pastor who is a true servant, committed to serving the flock and those working with him, can bring the peace of His government into the assembly. The important thing is that there is a government where Christ is clearly visible as the Shepherd and Head. There was more than one bar supporting each wall, showing that leadership should be plural. This is the environment that can best provide the diversity and government of God to oversee and equip the saints. Where the intention of those who build churches is to make a name for themselves and build their own kingdoms, there will always be a lack in the government of God.

We are to maintain a spirit of unity with *all* believers; we are not to merely tolerate them, but truly love them in Christ. Unity is not possible without the overriding influence of His peace and love in our hearts, regardless of church structure. We are required to love and fellowship with *every* born-again believer. We are to build correctly, but we are never to abdicate the commandment to love and fellowship with one another in Christ, being united in proclaiming the gospel.

All boards, including the five bars, were covered with gold. This tells us to look for the Lord's nature in each other as we stand in our position in His body. The five bars were each held in their position along the walls by *pure gold* rings fastened to the boards. This teaches us that it is the *Lord* who sets in place and upholds the fivefold ministries He has chosen for the Church, and *each member* of the body is to support them accordingly. Ministries are only effective as the Lord anoints them, and we pray for and financially support them.

The History of His House

Certain dimensions in the design of God's tabernacle in Israel result in specific areas that represent the three periods of time (or phases) of the Lord's house among men. The outer court was enclosed by walls which had a total surface area of 1,500 square cubits (Ex. 27:18). Counting one cubit for a year, this represents the amount of time between Mount Sinai and Calvary. During this period, God's house was in the tent, tabernacles and temples (i.e., Solomon's). The area covered by the holy place was approximately 2,000 square cubits. This represents the present 2,000-year period of the Church age, where the house of God is made up of living stones who are being built together in the Spirit. The area covered by the Holy of Holies is approximately 1,000 square cubits. This represents the Millenium Age, a period when His bride will tabernacle with Christ and reign with Him over the earth for one thousand years (Rev. 20:6-9).

The Pattern for Elders and Deacons

The Book of Numbers (Chapters 1, 3, 4 and 18) describes the appointment of men as priests to oversee and be responsible for the house of God. In this we are given a picture of how corresponding responsibilities for local expressions of the body of Christ are delegated to elders and deacons. The tribe of Levi was chosen by God to bear this responsibility of His house and, as such, they foreshadowed the ministry of elders and deacons who have the same responsibility for local churches. This tribe represented the *diakonate;* Aaron and his four sons represent the elders; their brothers who came from the same tribe were given to Aaron to serve by assisting and carrying out delegated duties associated with the tabernacle. They represent the deacons. Aaron and his sons were anointed by God to serve before Him in their priesthood, and they were commissioned to delegate specific responsibilities to their fellow Levites. The tribe of Levi in a total sense is a shadow of elders and deacons that serve each local assembly. The distinction between the two types of service are clear from the charge given by the Lord to Moses for the tribe of Levi. This is recorded in Numbers 18:1-7. Aaron and his fellow Levites were joined together as one priesthood, united in their service to the Lord and His house; however, the overall responsibility for sin against the sanctuary and ministry lay on Aaron's shoulders. He and his sons were responsible for the spiritual oversight of the house of God. Nevertheless, they could not fulfill the priesthood without their brother Levites. The same relationship in responsibility and function holds true for elders and deacons in a local church. There can only be a strong adequate eldership to minister the Word and provide spiritual oversight *if* there are men and women committed to supporting the elders and willingly responsible to undertake the multitude of services that are necessary for the functioning of a spiritual church. Together, they serve as a "corporate *diakonate*," committed to each other and committed to serve as *one man*, just as both types of priests were chosen from the same tribe in Israel.

The following illustration shows how the Levitical priesthood, in its relationship to the tabernacle, was a shadow of elders and deacons in the local church.

THE SHADOW

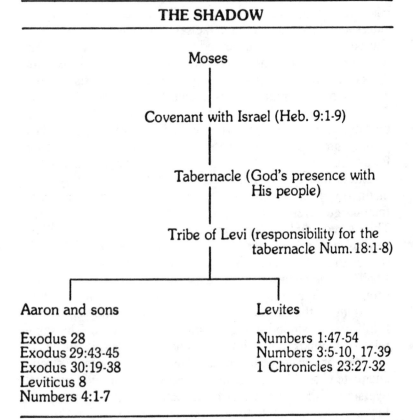

Moses
|
Covenant with Israel (Heb. 9:1-9)
|
Tabernacle (God's presence with His people)
|
Tribe of Levi (responsibility for the tabernacle Num. 18:1-8)

Aaron and sons

Exodus 28
Exodus 29:43-45
Exodus 30:19-38
Leviticus 8
Numbers 4:1-7

Levites

Numbers 1:47-54
Numbers 3:5-10, 17-39
1 Chronicles 23:27-32

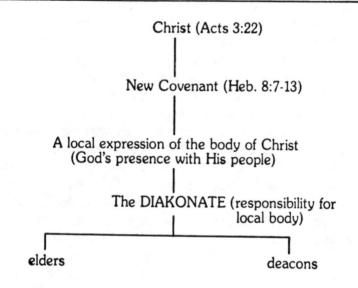

THE REALITY

Christ (Acts 3:22)

New Covenant (Heb. 8:7-13)

A local expression of the body of Christ
(God's presence with His people)

The DIAKONATE (responsibility for
local body)

elders   deacons

The following observations of the various functions assigned to Aaron and his fellow Levites also illustrate why they are a pattern of elders and deacons.

● The entire tribe of Levi (which included Aaron) was set aside from the rest of Israel as special to the Lord. They belonged to Him in place of all the firstborn in Israel; they were His to serve in the tabernacle, just as the *diakonate* is called by the Lord to serve His people in the Church (Num. 3:12; Num. 18:1-7).

● Aaron and his sons were ordained and consecrated for their office over a seven-day period. They were *anointed* with holy oil to set them in their priesthood. The Levites were *appointed* to their tasks (Ex. 29:7-35; Num. 4). Elders are anointed to shepherd, and they appoint deacons.

● The Levites were assigned to perform all tasks related to service of the tabernacle. They were literally "given to" Aaron and his sons to serve them so that the Aaronic priesthood could function as required by the Lord (Num. 3:6-10). This is analogous to the supportive functions of deacons.

● The garments that Aaron and his sons wore were for beauty, glory and holiness. The Lord instructed Moses how each item of clothing was a part of their consecration, for each piece was designed to express some significance of ministry. For example, on each of the two shoulder pieces of the ephod there was mounted an onyx stone upon which was *inscribed* six of the names of the twelve tribes of Israel. Over the heart, a pouch (or breastplate) was fastened which had twelve unique stones set in it, one for each tribe. Within the pouch, the Urim and Thummim, by which God gave direction to the nation, were carried. These picture for us the responsibility elders have to bear the burdens of the whole church and how their ministry of service must be from the heart for all the body. The Urim and Thummim speak of the responsibility elders have for the prophetic guidance and direction the Church receives (Ex. 28).

● As part of the consecration of Aaron and his sons, Moses was instructed to place some blood from the ram of ordination on the lobe of their right ears, on the thumb of their right hands, and on the big toe of their right feet. This speaks of the character required for elders: how they listen, what they do and how they walk (Ex. 29:20). Without godly character, elders become a failure in the Church.

• Aaron and his sons were responsible for any sin in the sanctuary or in the priesthood (Num. 18:1). Elders are responsible to deal with unrepented sin that is evident in the Church.

The Centrality of Christ

The tabernacle has many other related types and shadows of "good things to come" for the Church. These further picture the blessings and truth we can experience today as the Lord fulfills the reality of the commission given to Moses to build His house. Examples can be found in the various offerings and sacrifices, in the feasts, and in the clothing of the high priest.

However, I will leave these to the reader to search out and close with one final important observation. The tabernacle proper was not the wooden walls; it was a beautiful ten-piece curtain of fine twisted linen. This curtain, which was colored purple, blue and scarlet, had figures of cherubim woven into its texture. It was designed to cover each wall and the ceiling and to blend with the curtains of the two entrances (Ex. 26:1-6). No matter where one stood in the holy place or in the Holy of Holies, the beauty of this curtain was apparent about and above him. Since the walls were very tall and the articles of furniture relatively small, this curtain was always preeminent through its visible beauty. The curtain speaks to us of the central position Christ is to have in our life and growth. His righteousness is seen in the ten curtain pieces, which speak of the Ten Commandments He upheld and fulfilled. He is *always* to be the center of our attention; it is not our experience or our growth, but our relationship to Him that is supremely important. It is not the body of Christ but Christ Himself we are to seek after with all our hearts. Although He can be seen in the outer court in the form of the two curtains, the fulness of His beauty is visible only within the tabernacle.

In the same way, it is only as we see Him manifested in each member of His body that we begin to fully appreciate His beauty. He is to be the center of *everything* in the Church, just as the ten-piece curtain was so preeminently visible in the tabernacle.

Christ is not only central in the Church; He is also central in the lives of each of His children. This truth is expressed in type to us by the external structure and coverings of the tabernacle. The tabernacle proper was enveloped in three successive coverings placed upon each other in layers. These are representative of our body, soul and spirit. The outer layer was dark blue in color and made of porpoise skin. This is what was visible to those in the outer court (Ex. 26:14). The appearance was certainly not beautiful; it was dark in color and as a material was well-adapted to provide protection for the precious contents within. This outer covering is a picture of our body, which the Scriptures describe as a tent (or vessel) whose purpose is to contain the new man. There is nothing spiritual or beautiful in human flesh; only what is contained within has value in the kingdom. This covering could only fulfill its role through the death of the animals involved; similarly, the principle of death must be applied to our bodies if we are to reveal the presence and glory of God within.

The second covering corresponds to our soul. This covering was made of rams' skins that were dyed scarlet (Ex. 26:14). This covering came from the skin of an animal which was sacrificed for the forgiveness of sin. This fact, as well as its scarlet color, pictures for us the blood-covered souls of believers.

The innermost of the three coverings was made up of eleven curtains of goat's hair that were coupled together to make one overall covering for the wooden walls and tabernacle proper. This is a type of the human spirit. It is here in the heart that Christ dwells in each believer. The significance of goat's hair is that a goat typifies the character of our human nature (in contrast to the lamblike nature of Christ). The eleven pieces portray the following eleven virtues that need to be worked into our hearts by the Holy Spirit so we can contain the person of Christ in His fulness:

- poor
- joyful
- long-suffering (patient)
- pure (guileless)
- gentle
- meek (humble)
- temperate (controlled)
- faithful
- fervent
- peaceful (quiet)
- loving

In reality, this last attribute is the aggregate of the other ten virtues; since serving is love in practice, these qualities should abound in the *diakonate*.

This third covering was next to and covered the beautiful inner tabernacle curtain of purple, blue and scarlet. It encompassed that which signified the glory and beauty of Christ. In each of us, He is our hope of glory; He alone can bring the glory of God into our inner beings. This covering "contained" the beautiful curtain, just as our hearts contain Christ.

> ...*to whom God willed to make known what is the riches of this mystery among the Gentiles, which is* **Christ** **in you**, *the hope of glory.*
> Colossians 1:27

He is central in the Church, and He is central in us. It is not what we know or what we do that is important, but what He is in our lives.

*...that Christ may dwell in your hearts through faith; and that you, being rooted and grounded in love, may be able to comprehend with all the saints what is the breadth and length and height and depth, and to **know** the love of Christ which surpasses knowledge, that you may be filled up to all the fulness of God.*

Ephesians 3:17-19

As we behold Him in all His beauty and glory, we are better able to see the order and pattern of the work to which He calls us in His house.

Section Five

The End-Time Diakonate

THEME: We are living in wonderful days of restoration and transition in the Church. There is great anticipation of fresh visitations of grace and anointing to fall from heaven. However, these will be attended by greater testings and accountability to prepare the Church for the spiritual warfare and end-time harvest that are ahead. There is also growing apprehension of the rising immorality and economic problems which are sweeping the world. Great shaking is going on everywhere, including much of what has been conventional practice in religious realms. As a consequence of this changing environment, many questions are raised concerning the Church and her ministry. It is a day of decisions, for there are important issues that must be faced by leadership. Some of these concern the conflict of tradition with building a spiritual stature that will stand the the shaking to come. Spiritual authority is also an issue of particular significance. These subjects are discussed with an emphasis on those qualities that will be required to bring the Church victoriously through the perilous days of tribulation preceding the Lord's return.

Finally, as we move into the end-time we must be careful not to limit God. Although there will be great testings, there will also be great grace and an abundance of spiritual gifts and ministries. We are to believe Him concerning His promise of a restored Church with a restored gospel. The question is whether we will allow Him to bring us into the place He has prepared for us in His purpose.

Chapter Ten

Where Do We Go From Here?

The Next Wave?

We are living in changing times; not only are changes accelerating, but they are also more dramatic by their very suddenness. The recent changes in European communist nations is an example. The scenario of change being revealed in the house of God is precisely in step with these events in the world. He is setting the stage with new players, both in the leadership of nations and leaders of His people. All things to come in the world and the Church emanate from the hand of God and are totally in concert with His purposes for the last days of this age. Where we are today is exactly where He knew we would be when He created the world.

The charismatic renewal has been like a wave of the sea that rolled in over the shoreline and is now receding to the depths whence it came. It was cool, cleansing and refreshing to us, and we were delighted to play along the shore in the surf. However, there is another wave upon us which is much greater in its dimensions. We are going to be purified and tested in new ways. Any sand castles we have built on the shore are going to be swept out to sea. *Everything* we have built will be tested; a final shaking is coming over the land to bring down and remove all things that can be shaken, so that those things built of the Spirit, which cannot be shaken, will stand. We need not be ashamed if our faith is in Him and in the house He is building among us. It is a tremendous manifestation of grace and love from God that His people are given the opportunity to see what they have placed their faith in and to forsake that which has been built on sand and not on the true foundation. Only what is built with the *quality of His life* and *on Himself as the foundation* will stand the testings to come.

The charismatic renewal saw a gracious outpouring of spiritual graces and gifts to the Church. We are given spiritual talents, each according to our call, to equip us to build His house, to do warfare and to gather in His harvest. We are extended the privilege of becoming the first fruits of His harvest and being manifested in the world as His sons. We must not maintain the status quo, but seek the stature that belongs to the fulness of Christ. We are to grow up in *all* aspects into Him. Our limitations in the end will not be the things we want to do and can't, but the things we know we are to do and yet do not. We will not find our pursuit of the Lord's way to be popular, for we will encounter opposition from many whose hearts are like concrete, all mixed up and permanently set. Others will be tender and open to instruction. All reactions will be according to the foreknowledge of the Lord. The circumstances that we face in the days ahead are destined by the Lord to strengthen and prepare us for His purposes on the earth. We must be prepared to let go of things we have valued in the past. The future will be unlike anything we have experienced. What we have used in the past in the Lord's work may have no place in the future. As God equips us for His work, He must often strip us of useless tradition.

What About Tradition?

There are Christians who are very concerned with promoting the spiritual renewal of their tradition. They cannot imagine life in Christ apart from an established organization. They believe that genuine quality in any Christian endeavor must be superintended to be protected and sustained. They seek the comfort of knowing that all is "decent and in order."

Whether the tradition they endorse is Congregational, Catholic, Presbyterian, Episcopal, Independent or something else, they see only its renewal. To them, Christ is not building His Church; it already exists and merely needs to be renewed. The end result of this mentality is to conclude that the purpose of God is "charismatic ecumenism," rather than facing up to the demands of becoming the bride of Christ.

It is good for denominations and fellowships to work together, to reach out to one another in ecumenical overtures. When these good things occur, the Lord can speak and reveal Himself and His ways to people *right where they are*. It is not wrong to pursue these endeavors. Tradition is fine as long as it *does not* invalidate the Word of God (Mark 7:13). However, when the Spirit of God falls on His people as He is doing today, revealing His purposes and uncovering our carnal ways and sins, we *must* turn from them in repentance, both personally and corporately. It is wrong if we don't obey Him and press into the ways of His kingdom. A growing people is a changing people. It is wrong to be content with where we are; it is right to become what He calls us to be. This does not necessarily mean that believers are to leave their churches and seek for one with right structure and teaching; they are to seek Him and believe that as they obey Him and submit to His headship, He will build them together in a local body that is an authentic expression of His life.

It is when we look at the Church in geographic areas that we can truly see what the zeal for tradition has wrought. In localities everywhere the witness for Christ is crippled by the lack of unity between groups of believers, each one with its cry for orthodoxy. It seems that we have been more interested in showing why we are different than how we are the same in Christ.

It has been tradition for an assembly to own a building, not only for the facilities it provides, but also to express its identity as a church. If suitable accommodations can be rented, it could be a sin to bring the saints under the bondage of a large mortgage. Congregations should follow the same principles that individual members are taught to obey, one of which is to be free of debt. As much as possible, the Lord's money should be put into men, not into buildings.

There is need for a new vision and new priorities. The spirit of restoration that is being experienced today in scattered assemblies will one day be seen in His whole body. The Lord is not moving as He did yesterday; He is doing a *new* thing, and it is *not* renewing the traditions that have divided His body over the years. The mountain of the house of of the Lord is being raised up as a house of His glory. The "one new man" of His body is beginning to appear in the earth.

Building for Quality

Each man's work will become evident; for the day will show it, because it is to be revealed with fire; and the fire itself will test the quality of each man's work.

First Corinthians 3:13

Any quality of excellence in our walk and work can *only* come from the Lord Himself; yet each of us will be responsible for where we are found to be deficient. Things that look good do not always possess good quality; it is not a happy experience to find you have invested in a "lemon" when you expected to purchase a reliable car! Perhaps our spiritual life looks good to others, but how does the Lord see us? What will He find when He examines the assemblies we have built? How does one build quality that will stand the test of His fire?

We are taught in the Scriptures that the Lord is preparing a place for each of us in His Father's house (John 14:2-3). Although I have experienced no vision concerning this, allow me to suggest what we might see if our eyes were opened to what is going on in heaven concerning the fulfillment of this promise.

First of all, the beauty and glory of the city above would

far transcend anything we have imagined or expected. The center of everything would be the Lord Jesus Himself; all light and glory would emanate from Him. We would see myriads of angelic beings working and building beautiful "places" of habitation. These places would probably not be identical, but would exhibit varying degrees of glory. However, they would be harmoniously integrated into one magnificent structure.

The materials used would seemingly contain or reflect the many virtues and beauty of the Lord. Each such "place" (or house) would uniquely display His glory as a small but integral part of the great city that will one day be the future dwelling place of God among men. The finished city is described to us in Revelation 21:2-3, 10-23; 22:1-5.

It is quite clear that those who belong to Christ will one day bear His image (1 Cor. 15:49). However, it is also clear that we will *not* all have the same glory. For instance, we would not expect the thief on the cross who acknowledged Christ to have the same glory as the apostle Paul.

> *There is one glory of the sun, and another glory of the moon, and another glory of the stars; for star differs from star in glory. So also is the resurrection of the dead...*
>
> First Corinthians 14:41-42

Our glory in the age to come will be a measure of the quality of spiritual life we have attained while on earth. To put it simply, the Lord is building our house above with the spiritual virtues we allow Him to develop within us here. We send up spiritual material for Him to build with as we are being transformed into His image (2 Cor. 3:18, 4:16-18; 5:1-5). Those who overcome here will have a special place in that city to come made from the material they send up (Rev. 3:12).

When I allow the life and love of God to knit my heart to others in Christ, the quality of our fellowship and commitment will then be manifest in the spiritual structure of His house above. It is not only the fashioning of our individual lives that is important, but also how each living stone is fitted together with those adjacent to it. This bond of life between believers is how God has purposed, from all eternity, to build His habitation among men; the place of His rest where He will dwell for forever (Ps. 132:13-14). The city of God is in reality a home where the Father, the Son and His bride will be related together in the bonds of a family.

> *...In all wisdom and insight He made known to us the mystery of His will, according to His kind intention which He purposed in Him with a view to an **administration** suitable to the fulness of the times, that is, the summing up of all things in Christ, things in the heavens and things upon the earth...*
>
> Ephesians 1:8-10

The word "administration" is translated from the Greek word *oikonomia* which means literally "the law or arrangement of a house." The life bond of this arrangement in His house is what spiritual quality is all about. It is expressed by Scriptures which describe us as living stones who are being built together in the Spirit to form one body in Christ.

The object of maturity for an assembly is not to attain some structure of elders and deacons or to have great ministries. Such things are valid, but they are the means, not the end. Quality in the Church is expressed in terms of the fiber of His life that binds members together and how freely and effectively this life is presented to the lost and needy outside.

Your Place in the Body of Christ

Each child of God has been called to a place in His Church that no one else can fill. Each believer is special in His eyes.

I believe every Christian seeks the personal satisfaction of being fulfilled in his walk with God. However, it often seems too far above them and too difficult to attain. It is not something reserved for "the clergy." We can each become the person Christ calls us to be.

There cannot be true quality in a church unless each member attains his place in the purpose of God (2 Tim. 1:9). There are two simple ingredients in achieving spiritual fulfillment:

1. To *recognize and accept* our place in the body of Christ. To seek something else only brings frustration and conflict with others.

2. To *serve* others out of that place. Human instinct says fulfillment comes from being honored for what we have done or for who we are. This is not true; an abiding sense of fulfillment only comes as we lay down our self-centered ways and commit ourselves to serving others. Our motivation to do this should come from the call of God, not from trying to meet all the needs we see around us.

The Quality Control of Church Discipline

The physical health of our bodies is maintained, in part, by antibodies which fight agents of disease in our bloodstream.

In the same way, the Lord uses church discipline to deal with unrepented sin in the assembly. Sin that is not dealt with becomes a leaven that can corrupt others in the body. This is a day when God is judging sin in His Church in order to display His righteousness and power in her in the days ahead. Church discipline is appropriate only when one in sin will not submit to the Lord's discipline in his life.

Church discipline begins when the one at fault refuses to repent. His actions must then be brought to the attention of the church according to Matthew 18:15-18. This step, and any subsequent action, is a responsibility of the eldership, for it is an integral part of shepherding. All actions must flow out of the love of God.

Rather than cover all the details and implications of this difficult subject, I will simply list what I believe to be seven cardinal principles that should be followed.

1. Church discipline is *not* to be delegated. The overseers of an assembly are God's appointed watchmen to deal with issues of sin in the church.

2. Discipline should not be delayed in the hope that the guilty one may repent someday. To do so shows a lack of honor for truth.

3. Discipline should not be administered until it is clear that there is no repentance. To do so shows a lack of mercy.

4. Discipline should only be directed at the types of sin that require it, i.e., immorality, rebellion, repeated sin, heresy and sins of divisiveness (Rom. 16:17-18; 1 Cor. 5; 2 Thess. 3:6-15; 1 Tim. 5:20; Titus 1:10-16, 3:10-11).

5. Discipline is *always* to be redemptive and remedial in purpose. The Lord disciplines us because He loves us; this must be the heart of actions and attitudes both by the elders and the congregation. All actions must be bathed in the love of God.

6. Restoration of one who has been put out of the assembly must follow the same principle as the application of discipline. It must not be delayed too long or initiated too soon, and it must follow the fruit of true repentance as evidenced by a time of consistent behavior. Restoration to ministry should be considered *only* after restoration to fellowship. Restoration to leadership, if applicable, should be considered *only* after a period of time following restoration to ministry.

7. The assembly should *not* receive into fellowship one who is under valid discipline from another assembly. Likewise, if one under discipline leaves and goes to another assembly, the elders are responsible to communicate details to the leadership of that assembly. When an elder sins and does not repent, he must be confronted before the whole body (1 Tim. 5:20).

The Quality of Serving

As assemblies or individuals, we are obliged to preserve the unity of the Spirit. This obligation is not related to how we build or how far we may have grown in spiritual truth; it is based entirely on what we *are*: members of the one family of God through faith in Christ. We all have the same Father. By daily manifesting the character of the Lord in our relationship with other Christians, we can maintain unity of the Spirit with them. In other words, unity of spirit is based on what we are; what we *do in Christ* is related to unity of faith. Character, not doctrine, is the basis of unity. Paul expressed it well:

> ...*with all **humility** and **gentleness**, with patience, showing **forbearance** to one another in **love**, being diligent to **preserve the unity of the Spirit** in the bond of peace.*
>
> Ephesians 4:2-3

There are primarily five attitudes an assembly can have toward other churches in the area. I suspect these also represent different phases of our personal attitude over time as we grow up in Christ. I am sure we recognize that we will never serve others while we are in the first three phases.

1. *The "set everyone straight" phase*

This ungodly attitude is more common among cults than among believers, but I remember when I knew it all and couldn't understand why other Christians didn't see it my way. Perhaps some do not experience this mind set, but it is a common beginning phase for many of us.

2. *The "beat everyone" phase*

The objective of this equally ungodly attitude is to promote *your* church program. The action plan is to compete; the goal is sheep rustling. The rule is "do whatever is necessary" to draw other Christians into your assembly. The techniques are varied: use big-name preachers, advertise the meetings, build up the facilities, develop talented performers and use whatever promotional gimmicks will bring them in. Success is measured in terms of the size of the congregation and Sunday school. Quality becomes numbers.

3. *The "ignore them" phase*

In time we mature sufficiently to realize that competition in the family of God is contrary to the ways of the Spirit. Not knowing what else to do, we embrace an "ignore everyone else" mentality. We decide to go off by ourselves and build a "perfect church." We are the elite! Others will copy us (we believe). However, we only become a spiritual island. This phase produces little fruit, for there is no relationship outside the assembly. We are a contradiction to the body of Christ in the eyes of other groups.

4. The "serving phase"

Eventually we come to understand that whatever good things the Lord may have given us are intended to serve His people. It is a mark of maturity when we can embrace the principle of serving brothers and sisters who are outside our assembly. Once our hearts are stretched to see that we are called as one part of the whole body of Christ, we will cease being a closed community.

5. The "unity phase"

The last phase is a natural consequence of serving others; a bond of trust becomes established with other assemblies. It is now possible to give and receive ministry with them. This is a major step toward unity of faith.

Practical Considerations

What are some of the practical steps one can take to build unity with other assemblies in the area? Probably the most important requirement for an eldership is simply being committed to serve them as the Lord opens doors to do so. You cannot serve someone if you are competing with him; therefore, the first move is to lay aside any competitive sectarianism that may exist in actions or attitude. Obviously you cannot serve one who will not accept your service. Until we begin, we do not know who will not accept our service. Mistakes will be made; the Lord makes no allowance for our failures, but He does make provision for them through His grace.

There are numerous ways for assemblies to serve, such as sharing ministry, funding seminars, avoiding conflicts in the scheduling of meetings, sharing facilities, meeting in united prayer for the district, etc. The key is learning to trust and accept other leaders as His shepherds in the area. It will require much time and prayer, for only the Lord can bring it to pass. There will occasionally be ministry and religious activities which cannot be supported, but we should only stand against what is false and harmful. If we take these first simple steps, the Lord will make subsequent steps clear. The Lord asks no less in commitment between leaders on an area basis than He requires in local elderships.

The charter name of our assembly is "Fountain of Life." The Lord prophetically directed us *not* to build "Fountain of Life" as we reached out to serve the Church in this part of His vineyard. As a result, new assemblies that we raise up are *not* permitted to use our name, and their elders are *not* under our authority once they are set in place. In addition, our practice as the elders is *not* to tell the sheep what to do in their personal decision-making, but to *guide* them in making decisions according to the will of God. They must learn to know the voice of the Shepherd, and our role is to confirm His will. There are times when it is necessary to boldly speak directive words, but this should be the exception. These principles in building tend to dispel any authoritarian attitude that other churches might see in us as we reach out to them.

There will be an ever-increasing number of casualties from society: victims of drugs, crimes, broken homes and unemployment. The Church should see such persons as candidates for His kingdom. We will be surprised at how many will be open to the reality of God's love. Assemblies must learn to work together if they are to provide an effective sheepfold for these people. The heart of the Lord is set on raising up shepherds who will love and care for them and see them built into His house.

End-Time Shepherds

It is hard to see a picture when you are inside the frame. We need to stand back and view the Church as it concerns Him. Where His heart is points to where our commitment is to lie. His concern today is unfolded to us in Ezekiel chapter 34, which describes the consequences of a lack of good shepherding that over the years has resulted in the scattering of His sheep and in their spiritual poverty. Hear what He is doing about this condition today:

...Behold, I Myself will search for My sheep and seek them out.

Ezekiel 34:11

An evangelist will go out on the street corner and preach the gospel to everyone. Those who respond he will bring into the sheepfold. This is not how shepherds seek out the Lord's sheep. They look for walking problems: a bedraggled creature covered with mud and briars is often a problem with a back-slidden Christian inside. For example, economic pressures are often used by the Lord to surface those so burdened with debt that they can no longer go their own way. These sheep need His rod and staff to redeem and discipline their lives. Other problems will turn out to be sheep crippled by drugs, broken marriages, or sick from eating the poisonous weeds of cults. Still others will be gaunt from a diet of insipid social platitudes, empty liturgies and secular humanism. The Lord is raising up shepherds after His own heart to seek out His sheep and care for them.

As a shepherd cares for his herd in the day when he is among his scattered sheep, so I will care for My sheep and will deliver them from all the places to which they were scattered on a cloudy and gloomy day. And I will bring them out from the peoples and gather them from the countries and bring them to their own land; and I will feed them on the mountains of Israel...

Ezekiel 34:12-13

It is very easy and tempting for a successful ministry to gather sheep and build "a church." However, true shepherds will see that His sheep are established "on the mountain of the house of the Lord" in local expressions of His body. There will be many valleys that look good and are easier to enter, but only in the covenanted brotherhood of His house can the sheep be properly cared for. The paths of least resistance into valleys are not to be followed, for this is what makes men and rivers crooked.

I will feed them in a good pasture. ... There they will lie down in good grazing ground...I will feed My flock and I will lead them to rest...

Ezekiel 34:14-15

The Lord feeds His sheep out of His relationship to them. They know His voice, He calls them by name, He goes before them and has laid down His life for them. For that reason, they follow Him, and not strangers (John 10:1-16). Shepherds in the *diakonate* must pastor in the same spirit and with the same heart. This is the essence of the Lord's commandment to Peter, which He repeated three times for emphasis:

If you love Me, "Tend My lambs", "Shepherd My sheep" and "Tend My sheep..."

John 21:15-17

There is a difference between lambs and full-grown sheep. Newborn lambs are too weak to walk far and must be carried when it is necessary to move.

Like a shepherd He will tend His flock, in His arm He will gather the lambs, and carry them in His bosom...

Isaiah 40:11

Good shepherds will carry the weak and helpless near their hearts; they will be more concerned about the welfare of one lamb than salvation of the heathen. Above all sounds they will hear and respond to the cry of pain from a sheep that is hurt. This is why the Lord has divided His heart among the fivefold ministries in His house; evangelists do not hear such a cry, for their concern is for the lost. Young lambs do not see clearly and they are likely to eat plants that are poisonous. For this reason they must be fed what is good and be surrounded by those they can follow by example. They must not be left to wander off alone or be allowed to go their own way.

> *...He will gently lead the nursing ewes.*
>
> Isaiah 40:11

There is a temptation to order the priorities of our time so that we are more often with those who are spiritual and mature. Perhaps this is because we are personally strengthened by such fellowship. However, true shepherds will place their priorities on being with the lambs and those sheep with the greatest need. If there is not a proper concern in this matter, many weak or newly saved ones could soon disappear, for satan is always on the perimeter of the flock seeking whom he may devour. The Lord's concern as our Shepherd is first with the lambs and those who feed them, the nursing ewes. Pastors in an eldership are to manifest the same concern and priorities.

> *I will seek the lost, bring back the scattered, **bind up the broken, and strengthen the sick...***
>
> Ezekiel 34:16

A shepherd knows he cannot strengthen the sheep by subjecting them to legislated life in a barn. They must have room to exercise, sunlight to graze in, fresh water to drink, and exposure to the good pastures the Lord has provided on His mountain. He also knows the things that come into their lives are sent by the Lord to strengthen and make the sheep strong spiritually. For that reason, they teach the sheep how to walk through their circumstances, how to embrace problems, how to overcome, and how to avoid the cares of this life and luxuries that weigh them down. They will impart understanding of grace, repentance and discipline, which are necessary for sheep to grow and mature in the flock.

> *...I will feed them with judgment. ... Behold, I will judge between one sheep and another. ...Behold, I even I, will judge between the fat sheep and the lean sheep.*
>
> Ezekiel 34:16,17,20

The Lord becomes concerned when leaders begin to dominate the flock rather than serve them. I recall a prophetic word from the Lord that went something like this: *"I will come as the Shepherd of my flock, and I will go to the old rams; and if they let Me, I will break their horns so that they will no longer dominate others. I will go to the young rams, and if they let me, I will channel their zeal and energy into serving others."* If one in the *diakonate* ministers correction out of a harsh or bitter spirit he can hurt and scatter the sheep. His ministry is *always* to reflect the gentleness of wisdom from above (James 3:17).

An experienced shepherd discerns the false fronts and facades that sheep put on to hide their personal problems. Good shepherds are men given to confrontation out of hearts of love who will not run from problems.

Each shepherd carries a rod in his hand. One purpose of this rod is to test and examine the sheep as they come in and go out of the fold. They pass under his rod, which is used to examine their wool to ensure there is not infection or thorns on them.

> *And I shall make you pass under the rod, and I shall bring you into the bond of the covenant.*
>
> Ezekiel 20:37

In these days, each of us needs someone to love us, who will continually look into our life. One cannot afford to walk alone, apart from the flock of God.

The Lord seeks to remove the spirit of sectarianism from the heart of those He entrusts with the care of His sheep. Not ecumenism, but one body in Christ is His objective (Ezek. 34:23).

*And I have other sheep, which are not of this fold; I must bring them also, and they shall hear My voice; and they shall become **one** flock with **one** Shepherd.*

John 10:16

When we consider the role of leadership, we face questions on authority. How much authority does the Lord give elders over the lives of His sheep? What is the measure of authority vested in apostolic ministry? Spiritual authority is a more significant issue relative to end time events than most of us realize. Let us see why this is so.

Chapter Eleven

Spiritual Authority

Authority and Power

A country does not maintain law and order by allowing everyone to carry a gun with permission to use it as they see fit. We recognize the need for specific persons with authority to perform this task for the rest of us. Thus, we commission a police force and give them badges and uniforms to denote their authority. However, authority alone is not sufficient to enforce the law, should certain ones choose to disregard that authority. Therefore, the police carry guns. It is apparent that in the world, both authority and power must be present for government to be effective. The same is true for the kingdom of God; the government of Christ involves both His power and His authority.

Many Christians wonder, after receiving the power of God through experiencing fulness of the Holy Spirit, why the supernatural acts of God are not more evident among them. At first glance it seems that if every believer were filled with the Spirit, there should be a continuous succession of miracles until the forces of evil were totally dispelled. This is analogous to everyone carrying a gun — much power, but no directing authority. The Lord does not function this way, for His power is released as a consequence of His authority. In the Church His power is often withheld simply because His authority is not present in the lives or acts of those who would wield it. The following qualifying factors of power and authority will help us in understanding the human constraints that limit the hand of the Lord in the Church.

1. Although His power is boundless, we limit it by unbelief and a lack of seeing our need. His power is made perfect in our weakness (2 Cor. 12:9). As long as we are able, or believe we are able, to accomplish something solely by our own strength and ability, we will not experience His power in what we do. Apparently, this is a truth that most of us have to learn over and over again. Human confidence is a deceptive thing; our strength is to be found only in Him.

2. The Lord's authority, although total and complete, is not effective in the Church unless His people recognize and accept it. Thus, His authority is made perfect by our submission and obedience. The same is also true for any authority He has delegated. It is not how much authority I have that is important, but whether others receive it. Authority is not something that is developed within us; it must be delegated. All authority originated in the Father, and He has delegated it to His Son, the Lord Jesus Christ. He in turn, delegates it as He chooses in the Church. We see this in His charge to the twelve disciples:

> ...*All authority has been given to Me in heaven and on earth. Go therefore...make disciples...baptising them...teaching them...*
>
> Matthew 28:18-20

3. We need to distinguish between the words used for "power" and "authority" in the Scriptures. Power, or ability, is received from the indwelling Holy Spirit; it is translated from the Greek word *dunamis* (from which the word "dynamite" is derived).

> *But you shall receive **power** when the Holy Spirit has come upon you...*
>
> Acts 1:8

Spiritual authority, the right or privilege of position and action in the Church, can only come from the Lord Jesus Christ. This word is translated from the Greek word *exousia*.

*But as many as received Him, to them He gave the **right** to become children of God...*

John 1:12

*Behold, I have given you **authority**...over all the power of the enemy...*

Luke 10:19

All authority has been given to the Lord Jesus Christ; therefore we exercise delegated spiritual authority in His name.

The Authority of Christ

I remember as a young Christian that I received a revelation of the name of the Lord; I learned that His name carries the authority for everything the Church does in ministry. This was wonderful news to me; I was child of God and, therefore, had the privilege to use His name. I would accomplish wonderful things for Jesus; just be scriptural and do everything in His name! However, it didn't work as I expected. The revelation was correct; I understood who had the necessary authority and I understood how to speak, but I did not understand how to receive authority. I only had a formula.

Much of what is done in the name of the Lord is without His authority, which is one reason why such a ministry is so ineffective. We need to understand why the following verses of the Scriptures carry a *future* tense in their reference to the Lordship of Christ becoming a practical reality.

*But He, having offered one sacrifice for sins for all time, sat down at the right hand of God, **waiting** from that time onward **until** His enemies be made a footstool for His feet.*

Hebrews 10:12-13

*He is also head of the body, the Church; and He is the beginning, the first-born from the dead; so that He Himself **might come** to have first place in everything.*

Colossians 1:18

The Lord is certainly not waiting for satan or the world to surrender; He is waiting for the Church to accept His authority and allow Him to reign in her midst. The following Scripture yields understanding concerning this future aspect of His Lordship.

> ...*then comes the end, when He delivers up the kingdom to the God and Father, when He has abolished all rule and all authority and power. For* **He must reign until He has put all His enemies under His feet.**
>
> First Corinthians 15:24-25

If each of us surrenders the right to do his own thing (which is an enemy) and submits to the Lord's authority, He then can truly reign in His body and put all other enemies under His feet. The key is that He must reign! This involves not only His power, but also His authority.

The power of God rests upon the Church through the anointing of the Holy Spirit. However, His authority is extended to us in many ways both directly and indirectly as follows:

1. Each one in Christ has His authority to resist satan, and Christ reigns when we are obedient to do so (Luke 10:17).

2. Each believer (like Paul) can be personally called and given authority by the Lord for a specific ministry (Gal. 1:15). He reigns in lives that are obedient to such a call.

3. Authority resting upon ministries in the Church can be delegated to others (Titus 1:5, Acts 14:23; 6:3). Such delegation will *only* be valid *if it is recognized by those who it is intended to benefit* (2 Cor. 13:7-10). Furthermore, authority will be received more readily by others when it is exercised within a godly relationship rather than from an impersonal position of some office. The Lord reigns through His ministries as He builds His Church (1 Cor. 3:6-10). He reigns as we submit to one another and to those over us in the Lord. Thus character, not an office, is the basis of spiritual authority.

4. There can be authority inherent in one's place socially;

for example, the Lord reigns in secular lives when parents exercise authority over their children, when wives are subject to their husbands, and slaves (servants) obey their masters (Col. 3:18-22). Finally, rulers of the lands where believers live have their authority of government established by the Lord, and, except for laws that clearly contradict the Word of God, they are to be obeyed by the Christian community (Rom. 13:1-7). He reigns in our lives when we are obedient to those who rule over us. It is important to recognize that *all* of these areas of authority come out of the authority of Christ. One reason we are continually exhorted to submit to authority from childhood through adulthood, such as obeying parents, laws of the land, our employer, government officials, etc., is to cultivate a heart that easily bends before the will of the Lord. In God's eyes, rebellion against Him is no better than witchcraft (1 Sam. 15:23).

Jesus came as a servant; because He served obediently, He was exalted by His Father and given all authority. There is no better way for the men in the *diakonate* to exercise an authority that the saints will accept than by wearing the mantle of servants. People will respond more to the authority of a gentle spirit than to a loud, demanding voice. In fact, we only accept each other to the extent that we are subject to one another in the fear of Christ. Peter's exhortation sums it up well by encouraging all to clothe themselves with humility toward one another (1 Pet. 5:5). "Down" (humility, submission) is the way "up" (future place of honor). This principle is expressed in the following verses:

> *Blessed are the gentle, for they shall inherit the earth.*
>
> Matthew 5:5

> *Blessed are the poor in spirit, for theirs is the kingdom of heaven.*
>
> Matthew 5:3

That doesn't leave very much for those who are neither gentle nor poor in spirit!

The Christian's Authority Over Satan

The Scriptures are clear on our relationship to the realm and forces of spiritual wickedness. Before we were converted to Christ, we walked in sin and disobedience according to the influence of the prince of darkness. The following two verses describe the realm of authority we were under at that time:

And you were dead in your trespasses and sins, in which you formerly walked according to the course of this world, according to the prince of the authority [not power] *of the air, of the spirit that is now working in the sons of disobedience.*

Ephesians 2:1-2

For He delivered us from the domain [lit. authority] *of darkness, and transferred us to the kingdom of His beloved Son, in whom we have redemption, the forgiveness of sins.*

Colossians 1:13-14

Through conversion, we were totally removed from his realm, being transferred to the kingdom of God's Son. Satan has *no* authority over us in Christ, although he would make us believe the contrary. Once converted, the direction of influence is reversed; we are now called to overcome Satan through the strength of Christ.

Finally, be strong in the Lord, and in the strength of His might. Put on the full armor of God, that you may be able to stand firm against the schemes of the devil. For our struggle is not against flesh and blood, but against the rulers, against the authorities [lit. authority, not power], *against the world forces of this darkness, against the spiritual forces of wickedness in the heavenly places.*

Ephesians 6:10-12

We are at war with a realm of alien power and authority that is in heaven *between* us and God. If we become hurt by satan, it is *not* because he has authority greater than ours; it may be we have not availed ourselves of the Lord's armor in our warfare, or we have not been fully submitted to Him. The spirit of disobedience opens us to satan. This danger is much greater when we are not an integral part of a local body where there are those who can look after and care for us. James expresses the priority in this way:

Submit therefore to God [the first step]. *Resist the devil* [the second step] *and he will flee from you* [the result].

James 4:7

As evil continues to increase in the world many Christians ask, "What is going to happen; will the Lord rapture the Church and save us from the growing evil?" The answer to this question can be found in understanding the purposes of God for the Church in the great conflict that lies ahead.

The Conflict of the Ages

Three distinct phases of satan's authority are described in the Scriptures. The first phase is recorded in the book of Ezekiel, where the Lord, through the prophet, speaks to satan:

You were the anointed cherub who covers [lit. guards], *and I placed you there. You were on the holy mountain of God...*

Ezekiel 28:14

At this time, satan (or lucifer) was placed in authority by God over His creation, next in position to the Lord Jesus Himself. His authority was delegated to him and he was anointed with power for service. We know the story of how he sinned through pride and rebellion and was cast out of his place in the sanctuary of God. We are also familiar with his subsequent deception of Eve in Eden, and how he became the prince of this world through Adam's disobedience to the Lord.

The second phase began at Calvary, when the Lord Jesus came in the form of man and completely trimphed over satan.

When He [Jesus] *had disarmed* [or: "divested himself of"] *the rulers and authorities, He made a public display of them, having triumphed over them through Him* [lit. "through it, the cross"].

Colossians 2:15

The choice of "disarmed" appears to be a poor one in translating the word *apekduomai.* It means literally to "strip off or unclothe." The *New English Bible* translates this verse as follows:

He discarded the cosmic powers and authorities like a garment...

We now have a choice: to come under the authority of Christ or under the authority of the one in rebellion against Him by going our own way. The point is that satan still exercises authority and power over those not submitted to the authority of the Lord; in that sense he is not disarmed. However, he was totally defeated by the Lord Jesus, and from that time he has *no* power or authority over the Lord or His people unless we give it to him.

Indeed, the Church has been commissioned to rise up in the strength of the Lord and overcome satan. Since His ascension, the Lord Jesus is seated in heaven, reigning until all enemies are made a footstool for His feet. He is waiting for His body to come totally under His authority, so that as Head of the Church He will, in a *final conflict,* disarm and remove satan from his place as prince of the authority of the air. We are to overcome evil with the power and authority of Christ; the Church is destined to be victorious! The key of the future is the Church coming into the fulness of her strength in Christ. This involves more than being baptized in the Spirit for power. It means coming under the authority of the Lord Jesus. The body of Christ is to be in the earth as a conquering army (Joel 2) and as "a mature man" who is victorious over satan. The secret is Jesus; He must come to have first place in *everything* among His people; then He will do battle through His body. This is the second phase, the one we are in today. It is time of spiritual warfare, the conflict of the ages. It is worth noting that satan's strategy for this time is centered in the deception of the New Age Movement.

There is a time of travail coming upon the Church. She is now with child and soon to be delivered of a company people who will enter into this conflict against evil. This marks the beginning of the third and final phase, one in which the authority of Christ will fully come in the Kingdom of God on earth. We read of this in chapter 12 of the book of Revelation.

> *And a great sign appeared in heaven: a woman clothed with the sun, and the moon under her feet, and on her head a crown of twelve stars; and she was with child; and she cried out, being in labor and in pain to give birth...And she gave birth to a son, a male child, who is to rule all the nations with a rod of iron; and her child was caught up to God and to His throne.*

Revelation 12:1, 2, 5

We can identify this "male child" by referring to the following verses:

> *And he who overcomes, and he who keeps My deeds until the end, to him I will give authority over the nations; and he shall rule them with a rod of iron, as the vessels of the potter are broken to pieces, as I also have received authority from My Father...*

Revelation 2:26-27

This does not refer to one person, but to a company of those who overcome. After the "birth" of this company of people who are "caught up" to a place of authority, a great conflict will occur in the air where satan dwells between us and the Lord.

> *And there was war in heaven, Michael and his angels waging war with the dragon. And the dragon and his angels waged war, and they were not strong enough, and there was no longer a place found for them in heaven. And the great dragon was thrown down, the serpent of*

*old who is called the devil and satan, who deceives the whole world; he was thrown down to the earth...And I heard a loud voice in heaven, saying, "Now...the **authority of His Christ have come**, for the accuser of our brethren has been thrown down, who accuses them before our God day and night. And they overcame him because of the blood of the Lamb and because of the word of their testimony, and they did not love their life even to death.*

For this reason, rejoice, O heavens and you who dwell in them. Woe to the earth and the sea, because the devil has come down to you, having great wrath, knowing that he has only a short time.

Revelation 12:7-12

A summary of these verses suggests the following events:

1. A company of overcomers are brought forth from the womb of the Church into a place of authority before God. They apparently minister to the Church for a period of three and one half years (v. 5-6).

2. There is great conflict in the heavens, and satan is cast down to the earth (v. 7-9).

3. Because the heavens are then open, without the accusations and interference of satan, there will be great power upon the Church. The saints will overcome satan, even when it requires their lives (v. 10-11). The word of their testimony will carry the authority of Christ.

4. Satan's wrath will consummate in what is called the Great Tribulation. Before the Lord returns, all will be forced to decide for or against Christ; the Church in total will be purified during this time. There will be no gray, only white or black — righteousness or evil. There will never have been a time like this before on earth (Dan. 7).

The central issue is the authority of Christ. The Scriptures state that when satan is cast out into the earth, *at that time and not before*, the Lord's authority in fulness will rest upon the Church (Rev. 12:10).

The answer to our question concerning escaping tribulation is that through the strength of Christ we are called to overcome the evil of our day and be victorious as Jesus was. The Church is not to remain divided and weak; the way to victory begins with each member finding his place in the body of Christ, so that collectively we stand as "one man" in the authority and power of the Lord. Only in this way will He be Head of the Church *in practice.* We are being built together by the Spirit today to that end. This, not a pre-tribulation rapture, is to be our vision! The Church is at the center of all the events that will transpire, and we are to see His purposes in them. We can know the mind of Christ by what He is doing in our midst.

> *In order that the manifold wisdom of God might now be made known through the Church to the rulers and the authorities in the heavenly places.*
>
> Ephesians 3:10

Apostolic Authority

We can expect greater testings in the future and the proving of our Christian life and relationships. Many traditional Church concepts are being shaken; it is a day of transition and change. We are increasingly more conscious that we live in a day of new things. We recognize our need for a solid foundation as we face the future. The kingdom of God is not only in word but also in power. Therefore, it is not enough to have our understanding and doctrine reshaped; there must be a threshing out of new truth in our lives. We must have reality, not theory, as the basis of our walk in God. Just as there has emerged a greater reality in spiritual gifts, covenant relationship and discipleship, local expressions of the body of Christ, shepherding and the five ascension gift ministries, so also we can expect manifestations of the power and authority of Christ. I believe this decade will see a *great work* accomplished in and through the Church.

There is also going to be greater deception, with false prophets and counterfeit ministries going forth to deceive

those who are not anchored in Christ. As the Church is restored in fulness, so also will evil and deception come to a
fulness. The Church will be an ark of safety and protection
for the Christian. There will be many voices sounding from
the enemy's camp, but the Lord's voice will be one. It will be
clear and with authority. There are men being prepared in the
diakonate as trumpets of the Spirit to sound His Word throughout the Lord's camp. What the Lord is building is worldwide,
and there will be "ministries of communication" brought forth
to bridge between assemblies and localities so that we may
stand as one man. To this end we can expect to see greater
evidence of apostles and prophets.

The following are five areas where the authority of Christ
will be increasingly manifested by apostolic (and prophetic)
ministries, as the Lord builds the Church on an extra-local
basis:

1. Laying proper foundations for local expressions of the
body of Christ (1 Cor. 3:10; Eph. 2:20). Unfortunately, there
are innumerable struggling groups of believers that have not
established a suitable spiritual base upon which to totally
build their lives together. The fact that a man has fathered a
church does *not* qualify him as an apostle. The quality of the
foundation built in the church will prove his ministry. The
right foundation is simply Jesus Christ — not just He who
saves from sins and baptizes in the Spirit, but also He who
builds lives together, who develops godly character, who
governs, counsels and shepherds His people. This foundation
will involve a collegial eldership anointed to equip and shepherd the flock of God.

2. Hearing and proclaiming the Word of the Lord that is
pertinent to our time and circumstances. This includes iden-
tifying false prophets and counterfeit ministries as well as
warning of persecution and the implications of social and
economic happenings. I do not imply that such prophetic
words are extensions of the Scriptures, for the Bible is our
canon and must not be added to.

3. Working with other elders to equip the saints for service to build strong local bodies. The essence of maturity in the Church is the quality of life which exists in local assemblies and the spiritual bonds that exist between leaders of assemblies on local, regional and national levels.

4. Providing the spiritual ability and authority to bring redemption to assemblies that have lost effective local leadership, or who have fallen into sin so that they are a reproach to the Lord. (Apostolic ministries do not have a right to intervene in a normal assembly against the will of the local eldership.)

5. Training men just as Paul trained Timothy. Like Paul, they are to be spiritual fathers who reproduce their lives and ministries in other men (2 Tim. 2:2; 1 Cor. 4:15-17). The norm for *each* local expression of the body of Christ is that apostolic and prophetic ministries be raised up from its eldership and released to build His house on an extra-local basis. This is the reproductive principle of life by which the Lord builds His Church.

The Necessity of Authority

Men in leadership must recognize that it is always easier to *command* others than it is to *convince* them by setting an example. However, only by the latter is their authority in Christ effective. It is unfortunate that so many of the Lord's flock have been crippled and scattered over the years by ecclesiastical authority, not only from institutional bodies, but also from the dominance and charisma of leaders in sects and cults.

I know Christians who came from a dry, stifling, hierarchal religious background and, after experiencing the glorious life-flow of the Holy Spirit, now have an overwhelming concern to avoid any kind of spiritual oversight. They sincerely fear it would quench their new-found freedom and blessing. The reality of the joy and peace they now possess is too precious by comparison to their religious past to risk losing it. They see only their personal need for the headship of Christ; anything further smacks of the governmental constraints from which they have been delivered. Such people face a paradox: how to avoid authority while obeying the Scriptures that so clearly speak of spiritual oversight in the Church. They fear losing spiritual freedom if they submit to such oversight. This concern, in the ultimate, can lead such believers into a "just me and Jesus" mentality. The result, in a collective or congregational sense, is that they never face up to the call of Christ to be built together into a local expression of His Church. They prefer to remain a "prayer group," a people interested in seeking the blessings of God, but without a vision of corporate maturity. They do not wish to lose their personal independence.

As a consequence, they are more likely to eventually experience division and separation among themselves, since there will be a lack of those ministries specifically given to equip and build them together on a good foundation. They are also more vulnerable to error, or some unhealthy emphasis in teaching, because of the absence of effective shepherding in their midst. There are many groups who face this particular paradox today, and *it is a weakness* in the body of Christ. To correctly understand spiritual authority as Christ intends it, such people need to experience the strength, protection and beauty of the Lord when His authority is visibly present in a local *diakonate*. The Holy Spirit is moving everywhere today to establish the headship of Christ over *all* things in each Church. This is *never* to involve a chain of command to some distant place or person — only to Jesus.

The virtues of the Lord Jesus are unlimited; for example, His love, peace and righteousness are manifest as they grow in His people. It is the will of God that the glory and nature His Son, *including His authority*, fill the whole earth starting with the Church. The Lord will not force His authority on us; we are to lay down the right to exercise our authority and come under His. This is how He reigns — not by force, but by the willing submission of His people. Through those in obedience to Him, the Lord Jesus, as Head of the Church, delegates authority to certain ones in a church, *qualifying* them to exercise a sphere of responsibility which His Spirit *enables* them to perform. It is by this delegation of authority from Jesus that all valid ministries function. Certain delegated authority may, in turn, be delegated to others, but again *it will be valid only if it is received by those to whom it is extended*. In this way, apostolic ministries appoint elders, and elders in turn delegate authority to responsible men to function as deacons. In each case, delegation involves setting apart before the church those who are to *serve* others.

The Lord desires that man rule on the earth. This authority to rule was initially promised to Adam, who forfeited his right by disobedience. Eventually this promise will be fulfilled by those who reign with Christ. We will never qualify for that day if we do not learn both to submit to and to exercise spiritual authority now. It is always important to recognize the authority others have been given in Christ; anyone *with* true authority will be one who is also *under* authority.

Spiritual authority flows out of a spirit of *serving* and *submission*, for it is by living under the authority of Christ and those over us in the Lord that qualifies us in the eyes of God and the Church to have authority. It is said that one cannot claim to love God, whom he does not see if he cannot love God's children, whom he can see. It might also be said, "How can one say he is under the authority of Christ, whom he does not see, if he will not be under the authority of Christ's ministers, whom he can see?" True spiritual authority not only brings the strength and protection of the Lord, but it also reflects the beauty of His character. The Lord's authority was the result of His meek, compassionate heart of serving. It is a beautiful thing to manifest a spirit of serving, compassion, forgiveness, and to lay down "what we are" (or have) for the sake of others. This is especially important for apostles (1 Thess. 2:4-13). Such character is the basis of authority in the Church. When this is the case, we are more concerned with whom we *can* submit to than to whom we *cannot.* We need to realize that *all* authority in the Church, other than Christ's, is invalid, and His authority can only be established as we lay ours down and submit to Him, and thereby to one another.

A Light to the Nations

Each child of God is called to be a light to the world. From a historical point of view it can certainly be said that a multitude of tiny lights have always shone in the darkness. Each light has been a testimony of righteousness in the life of a saint.

I believe a significant change is coming. As the Church is built and comes into maturity in the days ahead, she will become one great light in the deepening darkness covering the world. It is a light that will draw multitudes into the kingdom at that time because of the glory of God resting upon her.

> *Arise, shine; for your light has come, and the glory of the Lord has risen upon you. "For behold, darkness will cover the earth, and deep darkness the peoples; but the Lord will rise upon you, and His glory will appear upon you. And* **nations will come to your light**, *and kings to the brightness of your rising."*

Isaiah 60:1-3

This light will be manifest in many ways: in the power of God through acts of the Holy Spirit, in the righteousness of saints, and in their unity and love for one another. However, it will also be "seen" in the authority of the prophetic word that will come forth to men, leaders and nations. The Church will be the voice of God to those who will receive it as He brings to pass His purposes among all men (Joel 3:14).

Let us consider the significance of this time of darkness as it will apply to the Church.

Chapter Twelve

The Lord's Return

Thy Kingdom Come

There is a great need among the people of God to prepare themselves for their Lord's return. Many seem unaware of the events that must first come to pass and are even now appearing on the earth. I have often wondered how godly men in the past prepared their charges to face extreme persecution and hardship. Surely the best counsel is that given by Paul and Barnabas to strengthen those early Christians who faced similar circumstances.

> *And after they had preached the gospel to that city and had made many disciples, they returned to Lystra and to Iconium and to Antioch, strengthening the souls of the disciples, encouraging them to continue in faith, and saying, "Through many tribulations we must enter the kingdom of God".*

> Acts 14:21-22

No one doubts we are entering perilous times. It is evident that the stage is being set for climactic events among nations, considering the economic power shift to oil-producing nations in the Middle East, the resurgence of Islam, the rise of terrorism, national and economic stresses. Values are changing, not only economically but morally and socially as well. Nothing is stable; there is no standard of righteousness; the priorities of yesterday are not the priorities of today, and they will change again tomorrow. Within the environment of such change and upheaval, Christians *must be sure of their foundation* and have their priorities and values properly set. The coming events are destined to have a great polarizing influence, for men will either be deceived and led into god-lessness or be converted to Christ. This is a day when *everything* is going to be tested in Christendom, and only what the hand of God has built will stand.

> ..."*Yet once more I will shake not only the earth, but also the heaven.*" *And this expression,* "*Yet once more,*" *denotes the removing of those things which can be shaken, as of created things, in order that those things which cannot be shaken may remain. Therefore, since we receive a kingdom which cannot be shaken, let us show gratitude, by which we may offer to God an acceptable service with reverence and awe.*

> Hebrews 12:26-28

In *no* way are we to be discouraged and fearful of the future. We are to be thankful, serving Him in faith, being assured that it is His good pleasure to give us the kingdom. Events coming to pass on the earth are intended to shake all things and leave only what has been ordained of God. In addition, we are to understand how the very shakings serve to prepare us for our place in His kingdom. In the future, this kingdom will fill the whole earth, a time that is initiated by the return of the Lord Jesus when He comes to be glorified in His saints and when they will possess the kingdom in its fulness (2 Thess. 1:5-10; Rev. 12:10; Dan. 7:18, 22, 27). These words of the Lord's prayer will be answered at that time:

> *Thy kingdom come. They will be done, on earth as it is in heaven.*

> Matthew 6:10

The Place of Suffering

What place does suffering and persecution play in spiritual growth and maturity? Some will say, "None; after all, Jesus paid it all for me, so why should I be required to go through such things? It would only be subtracting from what He has done for me at Calvary." It is true that Jesus did pay all of our debt concerning the judgment of God on sin. He has also delivered us from the authority of satan, so that we can walk in victory and righteousness through the power of His life. However, He did *not* remove the place of suffering and persecution as instruments of our maturity. Even though Jesus was without sin, it was necessary for Him to be perfected through what He suffered. Can we expect an easier way for ourselves? On the contrary, He has given us the example of how we are to follow in His steps (Heb. 2:10; Heb. 5:8). It is one thing to have our sins forgiven; it is quite another to be an overcoming Christian, and we are called to be overcomers. The following Scriptures make this abundantly clear:

> *For you **have been called for this purpose**, since Christ also suffered for you, leaving you an example for you to follow in His steps.*
>
> First Peter 2:21

> *And indeed, all who desire to live godly in Christ Jesus will be persecuted.*
>
> Second Timothy 3:12

> *And if children, heirs also, heirs of God and fellow heirs with Christ, **if indeed we suffer** with Him in order **that we may also be glorified with Him**. For I consider that the sufferings of this present time are not worthy to be compared with the glory that is to be revealed to us.*
>
> Romans 8:17-18

> *Beloved, **do not be surprised** at the fiery ordeal among you, which comes upon you **for your testing**, as though some strange thing were happening to you; but to the degree that you share the sufferings of Christ, keep on rejoicing; so that also at the revelation of His glory, you*

*may rejoice with exultation. If you are reviled for the name of Christ, **you are blessed,** because the Spirit of glory and of God rests upon you.*

First Peter 4:12-14

*And after you have **suffered for a little while,** the God of all grace, who called you to His eternal glory in Christ, will Himself perfect, confirm, strengthen and establish you.*

First Peter 5:10

No wonder Paul expressed a heartcry to know Jesus better in his words to the saints at Philippi:

*That I may know Him, and the power of His resurrection and the **fellowship of His sufferings,** being conformed to His death.*

Philippians 3:10

How often do leaders challenge the flock of God as Paul did?

For to you it has been granted** for Christ's sake, not only to believe in Him, but also **to suffer for His sake.

Philippians 1:29

Neither the Church nor we as individual Christians can come to spiritual maturity apart from persecution and suffering. If a newborn baby was placed in a sterilized room, kept completely free from contact with disease germs until full grown, and then released into the world, it would soon contract some disease and die. There would have been no building up of body defenses to overcome disease. It is the same with our spiritual defenses: We become strong only through overcoming. The promises of rewards made to the churches in Revelation chapters two and three were made to those who overcome. The heart of the gospel is our call from God to overcome and possess the inheritance provided for us by our Lord and Savior (2 Tim. 2:11-12).

He who overcomes shall inherit these things, and I will be his God and he will be My son.

Revelation 21:7

The Lord's Return

I believe the most significant Scripture containing details of the Lord's return is that given by the angels at His ascension (Acts 1:11). It does not reveal all the details, but it specifically identifies the *key factors* that mark His return. Let us examine their words and, in faith, receive the truth of what is so plainly expressed:

This Jesus will come in just the same way as you have watched Him go into heaven.

It will not be in the influence or form of the Holy Spirit that He returns, but it will be the same crucified and resurrected Jesus, the Son of God, who the first disciples had come to know and love. It was true that He would soon indwell them by the Holy Spirit; however it was not His presence with them in this manner that was to mark His return. He will come again physically to earth just as He ascended from it.

Because of this statement, we know the following to be true: He will return *visibly in the clouds,* and His return will be accompanied by the *presence and ministry of angels.* The following Scriptures provide further confirmation of this:

Behold, He is coming with the clouds, and every eye will see Him....

Revelation 1:7

For just as the lightning comes from the east, and flashes even to the west, so shall the coming of the Son of Man be.

Matthew 24:27

And I kept looking in the night visions, and behold, with the clouds of heaven One like a Son of Man was coming....

Daniel 7:13

And then they will see the Son of Man coming in clouds with great power and glory. And then He will send forth the angels, and will gather together His elect from the four winds, from the farthest end of the earth, to the farthest end of heaven.

Mark 13:26-27

For the Lord Himself will descend from heaven with a shout, with the voice of the archangel, and with the trumpet of God; and the dead in Christ shall rise first. Then we who are alive and remain shall be caught up together with them in the clouds to meet the Lord in the air, and thus we shall always be with the Lord.

First Thessalonians 4:16-17

And I looked, and behold, a white cloud, and sitting on the cloud was one like the son of man, having a golden crown on His head, and a sharp sickle in His hand. And another angel came out of the temple, crying out with a loud voice to Him who sat on the cloud, "Put in your sickle and reap, because the hour to reap has come, because the harvest of the earth is ripe."

Revelation 14:14-15

The Lord is not returning to rescue His Church from destruction, but to harvest what He has sown in the earth: a planting in righteousness that has ripened to maturity. He patiently waits for His harvest through the time of the latter rain which comes to fill out the grain so it might ripen into a good harvest. We usually associate "rain of the Holy Spirit" upon the Church with new anointings and demonstrations of spiritual gifts. While this is true, these are much less important than producing fruits of the Spirit in our character. Outpourings of the Spirit always bring fresh revelations of grace and ministry to the Church; however, when it is accompanied by persecution and sufferings, there is also more of the character of Christ manifest. The love of God shed abroad from hearts is what establishes the reality and validity of any revival. Revivals without the testing of hardships and persecution contribute little of permanence. It is fire that removes dross, and we are going to see much fire in the days ahead! The proof of our faith will be tested by fire at the end of this age. He alone must be the center of our affection if we are not to be ashamed when He comes. It is not visitation the Lord is seeking as much as habitation; He is coming to stay!

> *In this you greatly rejoice, even though now for a little while, if necessary, you have been distressed by various trials, that the proof of your faith, being more precious than gold which is perishable, **even though tested by fire,** may be found to result in praise and glory and honor at the revelation of Jesus Christ; and though you have not seen Him, you love Him, and though you do not see Him now, but believe in Him, you greatly rejoice with joy....*
>
> First Peter 1:6-8

Revelation 7:9-14 clearly states that the Church (described as a multitude that no man can number, the seed promised to Abraham) will be translated out of *the Great Tribulation.* This translation is the harvest of the Church. Harvest is a dramatic point in the life cycle of what is sown; it is the end of one phase and the beginning of another. So it is with the Church; we cannot enter into the fulness of the kingdom while still rooted to the earth. We must be harvested, but the Lord will not harvest what has not yet ripened. Farmers anxiously watch their maturing crops and the weather, until suddenly, one day, they know that it is the time to reap. The same is true for the Lord's harvest.

> *Now I say this, brethren, that flesh and blood cannot inherit the kingdom of God; nor does the perishable inherit the imperishable. Behold, I tell you a mystery; we shall not all sleep, but we shall all be changed, in a moment, in the twinkling of an eye, **at the last trumpet;** for the trumpet*

will sound, and the dead will be raised imperishable, and we shall be changed. For this perishable must put on the imperishable, and this mortal must put on immortality.

First Corinthians 15:50-53

Notice that this occurs at the seventh or last trumpet.

But in the days of the voice of the seventh angel, when he is about to sound, then the mystery of God is finished....

Revelation 10:7

The mystery of God is that we see and know Him as He is and will be changed into His image when He comes.

And the seventh angel sounded; and there arose loud voices in heaven, saying, The kingdom of the world has become the kingdom of our Lord, and of His Christ....

Revelation 11:15

In summary, although no one knows the day or the hour, the Lord Jesus will return at a set time, appearing in the clouds. He will be visible to all, and there will be angels present. When one of them sounds what is the last trumpet, He will gather His saints unto Himself, clothing them in immortality. We will have inherited the kingdom!

The Time of Tribulation

Many Christians are more occupied with interpreting the Scriptures concerning when He will return than with what they should be doing when He does come. To know what we are to be occupied with, it is imperative that we appreciate what is to take place during this period of time, what conditions we will face, and what purposes of God are to be worked out through them. Even a casual reading of the Scriptures reveals it will be a time of great tribulation, deception, persecution and testing. The Word of God is abundantly clear on this point. In our human weakness we can easily become fearful of the future when we consider the things that will come to pass. We are *not* to be fearful, but to be conscious of how much Jesus loves us and what He seeks to accomplish in the Church at this time. We are to be faithful to the vision of the "one new man," the body of Christ that is being raised up in the earth. Above all, we must be confident that *all* things are under His control. Where indifference and lack of commitment have been tolerated in the past, they *cannot* be afforded in this time of testing. The people the Lord eagerly waits for are His holy, spotless bride who has prepared herself (Matt. 24:1-13; Eph. 5:27; Rev. 19:7-8).

One truth we must recognize is that the Lord's return will be preceded by the appearance of antichrist, the man of sin or lawlessness.

> *Let no one in any way deceive you, for it* [the coming of our Lord Jesus Christ, and our gathering together to Him] *will not come unless the apostasy comes first, and the man of lawlessness is revealed, the son of destruction.*
> Second Thessalonians 2:3

> *And then that lawless one will be revealed whom the Lord will slay with the breath of His mouth and bring to an end by the appearance of His coming; that is, the one whose coming is in accord with the activity of Satan, with all power and signs and false wonders.*
> Second Thessalonians 2:8-9

This is a key climactic event of that time. The spirit of antichrist is already present in the world; however, this man will be the personification of evil. In Matthew 24, Jesus describes some of the conditions that will be present:

● Many will come in His name and lead many astray (v.7).

● There will be wars and rumors of war; nation will rise against nation (v.6).

● Believers will be hated, and some will be killed on account of His name (v.9).

● Many will fall away and betray and hate one another

(v.10). There will be great division among men in the world, but great bonds of trust and love will be established between hearts in the Church.

● False prophets will arise and mislead many (v.11); tares will be gathered into bundles to eventually be burned.

● Lawlessness will increase (v.12). Events will have a great polarizing effect on the hearts of mankind; many people's love will grow cold, but those who are His will be pressed into His love by the circumstances that surround them. There will be a great manifestation of the love of God within the Church, and we will learn to love those who persecute us. We will not be able to judge them if we cannot first love them in Christ. We mature through the things we suffer.

> *By this, love is perfected with us, that we may have confidence in the day of judgment; because as He is, so also are we in this world.*

> First John 4:17

● There shall be great tribulation such as has not occurred since the beginning of the world (v.21).

False christs will arise and show great signs and deceptive wonders (v.24).

In His admonition, Jesus emphasizes two things in particular:

1. The one who endures to the end shall be saved (v.13).

2. We are to believe *no* report that He has returned in secret (v.26).

> *But immediately after the tribulation of those days...the sign of the Son of Man will appear in the sky...and they will see the Son of Man coming on the clouds of the sky with power and great glory.*

> Matthew 24:29-30

Some believe the blessed hope is the return of Jesus to rescue us from tribulation. In reality, the blessed hope is that when He comes He will find us like Himself, a people of righteousness (Titus 2:11-14).

> *Beloved, now we are children of God, and it has not appeared as yet what we shall be. We know that when He appears we shall be like Him, because we shall see Him just as He is. And everyone who has **this hope** fixed on Him **purifies himself**, just as He is pure.*
>
> First John 3:2

The book of Daniel, which provides a similar picture of end-time events, reveals that many saints may be required to lay down their lives:

> *I kept looking, and that horn [antichrist] was waging war with the saints and overpowering them...And he will speak out against the Most High and wear down the saints of the Highest One, and he will intend to make alterations in times and in law; and they will be given into his hand for a time, times, and half a time.*
>
> Daniel 7:21, 25

Chapters twelve and thirteen of the Book of Revelation also describe this period of trouble. The twelfth chapter pictures the Church as a woman being persecuted by satan who is ministered to and helped during this persecution (possibly by overcomers and angels). The thirteenth chapter provides a vivid picture of the authority exercised by antichrist. His authority will be accepted by all who have refused to come under the authority of Christ.

The magnitude of evil and tribulation during this time is a direct result of satan's having been thrown down to earth from the place he now occupies in heaven. The bringing down of satan onto the earth marks the climax of his evil works among mankind; but it also means a time of great power upon the Church, since the heavens will then be open and free of his influence. Today he dwells between us and

God, where he constantly accuses us day and night. He is the prince of the authority of the air with domains of satanic influence over geographic areas, each under demonic leaders (Rev. 2:13; Dan. 10:13, 20). He is the god of world systems. The Church has been called to overcome him; this will finally take place with Christ's return at the end of the tribulation period. Thus, during this time of satan's wrath he knows he has but a short time, and in anger and frustration he persecutes the Church (pictured as the woman in Revelation 12:13-17). When he appears he will have apparent answers for the economic and political issues facing nations. However, he will deceive all who embrace him and his proposals.

An unfortunate word choice in most translations of Second Thessalonians 2:7 has led some to believe that the Holy Spirit (and thus the Church) will be taken out of the earth prior to the appearance of antichrist. This is not so. The word of concern is *ginomai*, which is translated many times in the New Testament as "to come into being or to become," and only this once as "be taken." The *Concordant Literal New Testament* translates verses 6 and 7 as follows:

> *And now you are aware what is detaining, for him to be unveiled in his own era. For the secret of lawlessness is already operating. Only when the present detainer may be coming* **to be** [or is coming] **out of the midst.**

Satan, the accuser of the brethren, is the detainer. Paul had apparently explained previously how satan was hindering them as prince of the authority of the air. He was the secret, unseen spirit of lawlessness against whom they conducted warfare in the heavens. However, the day would come when he would no longer be a secret but *would become clearly manifested*, appearing in the midst of mankind in the person of the antichrist. Unlike God, satan cannot be in different places at the same time. He is not omnipresent. When he is cast down to the earth and is personified as the man of sin, he loses his place in the heavens. When Jesus returns, he then will also lose his place as the prince of this world.

Revelation chapter thirteen describes how the devil will reveal his power and authority through a satanic trinity of ungodliness. He is allowed to make war with the saints and overcome some of them (Rev. 13:7). The following verses illustrate the attitude and responsibility that Christians will be called to manifest at this time:

*And they **overcame** him* [Satan] *because of the blood of the Lamb and because of the word of their testimony, and they did not love their life even to death.*

Revelation 12:11.

Whoever is to be led into captivity will be led into captivity; whoever kills with the sword must be killed by the sword. In this way the saints exercise their endurance and their faith.

Revelation 13:10, *The New Berkely Version*

Martyrdom is not a pleasant thought to our humanity; however, the blood of martyrs has been the seed of the Church in many lands, and it will again be common in those days. (Revelation 6:9-11).

It may be difficult for those Christians who have been taught the concept of a pretribulation rapture to accept the fact that the Church is going to be present in the earth during the period of satan's wrath. However, the Scriptures assure us that we are **not** *appointed to suffer the wrath of God.*

For God has not destined us for wrath, but for obtaining salvation through our Lord Jesus Christ, who died for us, that whether we are awake or asleep, we may live together with Him.

First Thessalonians 5:9-10

"And they will be Mine," says the Lord of Hosts, "on

> *the day that I prepare My own possession, and I will spare*
> *them as a man spares his own son who serves him."*
>
> Malachi 3:17

It matters not whether we lay down our lives for Him (be asleep), or live through this period of trouble (be awake), for we abide in Him and He in us, and He will *never* forsake us. Indeed, His judgments will not fall in final wrath until He has come and taken us to Him, so that His body can participate with Him as an army in cleansing the earth (Jude 14:15; Rev. 19:11-15; Mal. 4:1-3; Is. 13:3-13; Joel 2:1-11; Zech. 14:3-5; Ps. 149:5-9).

I would encourage readers to consider prayerfully chapters six through fifteen of the Book of Revelation as not being one continuous chronology of events, but rather three different symbolic presentations of those events that will occur in the period just prior to and including the Lord's return. The seven seals (Rev. 6 and 7) are one such picture; the seven trumpets (Rev. 8, 9, 10 and 11) provide the second and Rev. 12 through 15 provide the third. Different details and events are pictured, but the heart of each of these symbolic revelations given to John is the Lord's coming for His Church. The following verses show this threefold, repetitive description of His return:

1. Rev. 7:9, 14-15
2. Rev. 10:7; 11:15-16 (See 1 Cor. 15:51-52; 1 Thess. 4:16);
3. Rev. 14:13-16.

The Purposes of God

We are not to think of the days ahead as a time when satan does his thing, and then God tries to salvage what He can out of the mess. On the contrary, this period of time is a consummation of the Lord's plan of salvation for the end of this age. It is the time when we enter into our inheritance in the kingdom and rule with Him during the Millennium. We must be open to the purposes He will bring to pass in the

Church at this time. It gives great peace to know that *all* future events have their place in the Lord's building of His Church. Our vision, theology and ministry are to be shaped by the purpose of God, not the many needs that we see around us. He is raising up members of His body to be instruments of the Spirit, each according to the anointing He gives them. Many are being apprehended and prepared to build the house of the Lord. Those who are open and receptive today are being built together as living stones in this glorious house. Some, who are not open now, will be in the circumstance of the future.

The story of Joseph provides us with a type or shadow of this ministry. Joseph was the key in the purposes of God for his day. He was given revelations of a future role he was to have that concerned his brethren. However, when Joseph made his revelations known to them, his brothers despised him; out of pride and envy they cruelly separated him from their midst and sold him as a slave to some Egyptians. He went through approximately twenty years of testing in Egypt where he overcame all temptations to deny his integrity, his call, and his God. He proved himself through adversity and persecution as well as in periods of honor and fame. His total life was proven, both secular and spiritual. Through the anointing upon him, Joseph prepared himself and those for whom he was responsible to survive the seven years of famine that came upon the earth following a period of great abundance.

Once again God is preparing "Joseph sons." Like Joseph, we are to understand the significance of the great abundance of spiritual life that is being poured out by the Holy Spirit today and know how to store it in the granaries of our hearts. This supply is necessary to preserve and minister life in the days of famine that lie ahead for His people, especially to those who have not entered into the abundance of today.

Joseph never lost his love for his brethren; when they came to Egypt for corn, he went aside and wept for them.

Later, when they returned to receive the food they required, Joseph identified himself to them and revealed what was the key to their redemption:

> *And now do not be grieved or angry with yourselves, because you sold me here; for God sent me before you to preserve life. ... And God sent me before you to preserve for you a remnant in the earth, and to keep you alive by a great deliverance.*

Genesis 45:5, 7

Those who are being called out of sleeping churches into local expressions of His body are to have the same love and provision for their brothers in Christ they have left behind that Joseph did for his brothers. Joseph is not a type of "super minister," one with a superiority complex. He is an example of those who serve their brothers.

The question is, how do we become a "Joseph son"? Just as Joseph was chosen by revelation and prepared to minister to his brethren in the time of famine, there is also a company of sons today whose hearts have been opened by the Lord and who are being prepared through testings for His purpose during the coming tribulation. There will probably be severe restrictions on public ministry of the Word at that time. Although it may be underground, great ministry will be needed to protect and strengthen the Church. Ministry in the power of the Holy Spirit, along with the testing of persecution fires, will bring about a purification of the Church. This company of sons is described in the Scriptures as a "Man child" and as "overcomers" (Rev. 12:5; Rev. 14:1-15). The "man child" is in the womb of the Church, soon to be birthed — the event that is related to bringing down satan from heaven.

There are many whose hearts thrill with visions of the final glory of the Church. By faith, they see the "one new man" that will stand upon the earth, made up of all races, Jew and Gentile, the body of Christ which is the fulness of His magnificent person. Like Joseph, they too have found themselves separated from certain Christian brothers because of their revelations. In place of this lost fellowship, they are experiencing greater depths of spiritual commitment and relationship in local, free-flowing expressions of His body. These are springing up around the world as part of His house which is being built for a place of supply and safety in the days of trouble ahead.

For in the day of trouble He will conceal me in His tabernacle....

Psalm 27:5

We must love the house of God. Like Joseph, we are to have a heart of love for all of our brothers in Christ; however, we must also be willing to be separated from some of them for a season *if* the Lord wills it so. It is infinitely more important that our vision be centered in the Lord's purpose for His Church rather than some lesser objective, such as building our personal ministry or the renewal of some organization. It is no small thing to which the Lord is calling us, for what He does in the Church will affect the entire earth, even as the ministry of Joseph did.

*And the people of **all the earth** came to Egypt to buy grain from Joseph, because the famine was severe in all the earth.*

Genesis 41:57

It is not God's blessing on the work of our hands that is needed, but our commitment to Him and His work. Only what He has built will stand the test of that day!

The record of Noah and the ark provide us with yet another type of the ministry related to the purposes of God in this period of time.

For the coming of the Son of Man will be just like the days of Noah.

Matthew 24:37

The world will not understand the significance of the body of Christ in these days any more than it understood the ark of Noah. The key to salvation in that day of judgment was to be found in what was being visibly built for all to see. It was seen but not understood. The righteous Noah and his family were not rescued out of the judgments of God. Rather, they dwelt safely in the midst of them. The secret of their deliverance was Noah's obedience to the Lord's direction in building the ark. Like Joseph, Noah's obedience made him a preserver of life on the earth. He could have saved his own life and his family's with a much smaller boat. However, he fulfilled the purposes of God by building *exactly* to the pattern given him by the Lord. It is the same today. The pattern has been given, and we had better build according to it if our work is to stand the shaking to come and be used to preserve life on the earth! The *only* building that will stand in that day is the house of the Lord. Like Noah, we have to build for times and conditions that we have never before seen or experienced.

There are many facets of the Lord's life that go into building the "ark of God." The heart-to-heart fellowship and "committed-togetherness" of the Lord's people arise out of His total commitment to each one of us. Our commitment must also be total as we reach out to one another. We must learn to help one another in the practical economics of everyday life as well as in the ministry of spiritual things. We can expect the Lord to raise up men and women with understanding of how the body of Christ can be more independent of the world's system of commerce. There will be famines and shortages of much that we consider necessary today for livelihood. We will learn to live with what are truly necessities and to share our sustenance with one another. What the Lord provides will always be sufficient *when we live within the ordained relationship of His body*. The Lord will use the events of those days, both privation and supply, to establish us as the one body we are called to be. However, I am not suggesting that all will be called out of metropolitan areas into the country-side. How He leads us will be unfolded as we focus on that which is primary: to be built together in the Spirit as living expressions of His body right where we are.

What Will You Be Doing?

What will you be doing when Jesus returns? It will be the time when He settles accounts with His servants who have been given talents according to their abilities. Those who have multiplied their graces and gifts will be entrusted with authority in the age to come (Matt. 25:14-29). The day of His coming will consummate a time of testing, harvest, purification and final victory for the Church. The spots and wrinkles, so common today in the Lord's body, will be gone when He returns. He is coming to be glorified in His saints. The burden of leaders is to prepare the saints to be overcomers in this time of glory for the Church, a time when she is presented to her bridegroom to possess the kingdom prepared for her from the foundation of the world (Rev. 19:7; Matt. 25:1-10).

If we can see the purposes of God for this period of time, I believe there are seven things in particular to which we should give ourselves. Implicit in each one is our personal total commitment to the Lord Jesus Christ.

1. We will seek to avoid deception.

...See to it that no one misleads you. For many will come in My name, saying, "I am the Christ," and will mislead many.

Matthew 24:4-5

...The Spirit explicitly says that in later times some will fall away from the faith, paying attention to deceitful spirits and doctrines of demons.

First Timothy 4:1

When we are grounded in truth and have a protective relational covering of brothers in the Lord, plus a sure relationship in Christ, we need not fear deception. In assemblies, members of the *diakonate* are to stand as watchmen on the wall warning the sheep of all that is false and what they see coming to pass that would be harmful.

2. We will avoid indifference and lukewarmness:

And because lawlessness is increased, most people's love will grow cold.

Matthew 24:12

One of the key blessings of body life is the informal environment that stimulates the mutual encouragement of one another in Christ. It is out of this quality of relationship with another that we are free to call continually and challenge each other to greater commitment. Circumstances of the future will dictate even more the need for home group meetings. We must not forsake the assembling of ourselves together and all the more as we see the day drawing near (Heb. 10:25).

3. We will build relationships in families, local assemblies and between assemblies that will stand the pressures and temptations of that time.

And at that time many will fall away and will deliver up one another and hate one another.

Matthew 24:10

The deceptions of that day will seek to turn children against their parents; hypocrisy and betrayal will be the trend of society (Matt. 10:21). In contrast, there will be a drawing together in the body of Christ, and unity will mark the Church of God. What we speak of as unity in a conceptual sense today will become a reality then.

4. We will seek to avoid the "little things" that by their legality and subtlety can so easily usurp our time from that which is necessary. The greatest protection against such things and the forces of darkness is constant attention to prayer.

Be on guard, that your hearts may not be weighted

down with dissipation and drunkenness and the worries of life...But keep on the alert at all times, praying in order that you may have strength to escape all these things....

Luke 21:34, 36

Additionally, we must not be conformed to the social patterns that will exist. In order to be prepared, we must begin to cut those tentacles of this world system that will drag us down into the confusion of that day. In particular, we must be free of debt and, as the Lord leads us, become less dependent on the world's system of commerce (Rev. 13:17). This is already beginning to take place in churches across the land.

5. We will be our brothers' keepers, for understanding brings with it greater responsibility.

And those who have insight among the people will give understanding to the many; yet they will fall by sword and by flame, by captivity and by plunder, for many days. Now when they fall they will be granted a little help, and many will join with them in hypocrisy. And some of those who have insight will fall, in order to refine, purge, and make them pure, until the end time; because it is still to come at the appointed time.

Daniel 11:33-35

6. We will have a heart for evangelism, especially for the poor.

And this gospel of the kingdom shall be preached in the whole world for a witness to all the nations, and then the end shall come.

Matthew 24:14

There will be a great harvest of souls during this period of tribulation, even while there will be many who fall away from the faith. All mankind will be brought to a place of decision in that day.

The sun will be turned into darkness, and the moon into blood, before the great and awesome day of the Lord comes. And it will come about that **whoever calls** *on the name of the Lord will be delivered....*

Joel 2:31-32

The Lord will work in ways we cannot imagine to bring multitudes from the nations into His kingdom (Joel 3:13-14; Is. 60:1-5). It will be time of great ingathering, and Israel will not be forgotten. This period of history will mark the end of the fulness of the Gentiles. The spirit of grace will bring a remnant of Israel into the Church (Rom. 9:27, 11:5, 25; Zech. 8:11-12; 13:8-9; Micah 5:3-5).

7. Finally, we will not attempt to stand alone as individuals in that day, but as members of the body of Christ. We will need each other as never before. Victory will lie in our personal and corporate relationships to Christ. It is this relationship that we are called to build and establish today. We are to comfort, encourage and build up one another so we can stand as *one man,* even as His army in the earth. The people who know Him in this sense will be strong and do exploits in His name. They will be a people who have been trained and disciplined to move as one in the strength and armor of God. They will march to the sound of worship and praise, for the victory will be theirs!

*Therefore, take up the full armor of God, that you may be able to resist **in the evil day,** and having done every-thing, to stand firm.*

Ephesians 6:13

I see no ministry today greater than being committed to fill our place in the body of Christ and to see the Church equipped and come into the place to which she has been called to by her Lord. To serve one another, to share our life, to encourage and strengthen our brother may not seem as glamorous as casting out demons, but the consequences can be much more significant.

Encourage the exhausted, and strengthen the feeble.
Say to those with anxious heart, "Take courage, fear not.
Behold, your God will come with vengeance; the re-
compense of God will come, but He will save you."

Isaiah 35:3-4

Our humanity always looks *back* to our "spiritual gene-alogy" and tradition; the devil always points us *back* to our sins and failures. However, the Lord directs us to the *present* and the *future* and encourages us to put away our thoughts of the past. We are exhorted by Paul's own testimony to have this attitude.

*...**Forgetting what lies behind** and reaching forward*
to what lies ahead, I press on toward the goal for the prize
of the upward call of God in Christ Jesus.

Philippians 3:13-14

We *cannot* build on yesterday's vision. This would, of course, be far more comfortable and less demanding of our faith. However, we are called to walk a new way, one for which there are not many footsteps marking the path. It is to be a walk of continuing revelation. Accompanying the pressure of circumstances in our personal life, the national distresses we experience, the many temptations of our society, and the manifold growth of evil and sin in the land, there is a growing sound of an abundance of rain! The Lord is preparing the Church for His return; not a weak, divided Church seeking rescue from evil, but one standing united in power and victory. This is my vision.

Conclusion

To whom much has been given, much will be required. There is an accountability that is inherited with spiritual responsibility. The most privileged people in the earth today are those to whom God has entrusted the gifts and graces of the Holy Spirit. As a consequence, they stand with great responsibility before Him; a responsibility, not to perform, but to obey.

The charismatic renewal saw much truth restored in the areas of spiritual ministry, body life, discipleship and shepherding. However, this understanding only remains a concept unless it is put into practice in local expressions of His life. And wonder of wonders, when this is done, out of the informal atmosphere of small cell or home groups we begin to see what "church" is all about — real joy and love, with a care and commitment that can be found only in the body of Christ. People become bonded together as living stones by the fiber of His life. Worship takes on new meaning. Members find their places of service in the body, and servants are raised up to serve and oversee the house of the Lord.

As the Church is restored according to the pattern of the early Church, we are increasingly faced with diminishing options as to how to build. Many traditional practices and values are no longer valid. A prophetic people will be a people of change. We must be willing to make transitions. The authority levels in church structures must be replaced by collegial groups of men with hearts to serve.

Revivals of the past have always left a heritage of truth that believers have supported as doctrine, often without having a continuing reality of those truths. We have always looked back to the "good days" of past experiences. How can this be avoided in the restoration of today? I believe we bear a great responsibility to obey and walk in the truths of this hour. Healthy organic cells continue to reproduce themselves; healthy cells of spiritual life do likewise. We need not lose the vitality of His life that has been so graciously given to us. The Church should grown in strength and reproduce herself until she becomes that light in the world that the Lord intends her to be. For this to happen, multitudes must be apprehended by the Spirit for their place in the *diakonate*. Servants are required to plant, build and oversee local expressions of the body of Christ.

Would a Christian family send their young children away to someone else for training? The answer is "no," for the bonds of family love forms the God-ordained environment in which to train them. It does not matter that more knowledge may be concentrated in a school, because family life is needed to mold their characters. Similarly, the spiritual resources within a body of committed believers, in concert with traveling ministries, provide the ideal "home environment" for training disciples. A regimen of secular work, and the fellowship, sharing and teaching activities of body life, offer an excellent school of the Spirit. Conventional education is valuable for certain subjects when specific needs arise; for example, good homiletics, communication, learning a trade, etc. However, the final qualifications of a valid ministry is not based on academics but on quality of spiritual life that is imparted to others.

In closing, I have great anticipation of what lies ahead. I believe there will be a continuing ascension of spiritual gifts and graces from the Lord in new dimensions of ministry in order to prepare His bride and bring in a great harvest of souls. I therefore encourage all who God has called into His service to prayerfully consider what I have presented. Let us arise and build.

Crucible of the Future by Dale Rumble. Here is an incredible look into the 1990's by a former IBM futurist. In this book, the author turns his attention to the world of the future as it relates to the Church's triumphant but costly role in the last generation of this age. The Church will face the most challenging test ever of her devotion to the Lord, her purity and her real supernatural power. It is a glorious picture of restoration in the mist of international turmoil. TPB-168 p. ISBN 0-914903-89-6 Retail $6.96

Prepared for His Glory by Dale Rumble. What is it that really prepares a man for God's glory? In this book, Dale Rumble gives us a fresh view of what God is doing in the Church, as well as what lies ahead for His people. God's intention is for His glory to be intricately woven into the fabric of who we are as men and women. This is expressed simply in words and vivid graphic illustrations. This is a foundational and preparatory manual for this generation of Christians who will abandon all to follow Christ. TBP-288 p. ISBN 0-914903-08-X Retail $8.95

Winds of Change by Donald Rumble. "The greatest mistake," wrote A. W. Tozer, "is to resist change." Nonetheless, such resistance appears endemic to human nature. This booklet was written to challenge believers to respond to the Lord in these critical times of change. A whole new realm of spiritual life and truth awaits all who will be truly open to God's moving, as He leads us to change from one degree of glory to another. PB-72 p. ISBN 0-914903-12-8 Retail $2.95

The Ephesian Connection by Donald Rumble. This book is a prophetic call for God's people to make the connection! The Ephesian Connection begins with heart-felt repentance and a resolve to live in intimate communion with the Lord Jesus. It is only when this happens that the Church will discover who she really is and will bring to this generation the power of the ages to come. TPB-210 p. ISBN 1-56043-016-8 Retail $5.95